TIME AND TIMELINESS

TIME AND TIMELINESS

by H. I. MARROU
translated by Violet Nevile

SHEED AND WARD : NEW YORK

CONTENTS

In other words, all authentic history is salvation history.—A. D. Sertillanges

There is only one history, that of humanity on its way to the kingdom of God, this is the true "salvation history."—E. Mounier

We are living in the midst of the history of salvation.
—J. Daniélou

TIME AND TIMELINESS

PART ONE

PART ONE

1. THE MEANING OF HISTORY

Nearly thirty years ago when I was young and inexperienced I wrote a little book which I was bold enough to call, *A Treatise on Music in the Spirit of Saint Augustine,** in which I set out my ideas on the subject in the hope that, with the aid of such a title, the public would realize that they were invested with considerable authority. Today I would not dare to resort to such blackmail. What follows is the direct outcome of a long and persevering frequentation of Augustine's work and especially of his *City of God:* it has far more claim than that other to have drawn sustenance from his thought, and if there is any validity in my own reflections it is entirely thanks to Augustine's teaching. I have tried to make it possible for the reader to recognize this at each step of the way. In these pages, then, the reader will find what I have been able to learn in the course of a long career during which I have had the privilege of taking part, as one among others, in the scientific work of an international team of philologists, scholars and historians who, in this generation, have taken on the task of recovering and developing the thought of this great African Doctor of the Church, which is a part

* *Traité de la musique, selon l'esprit de saint Augustin,* La Baconnière, Neuchâtel, Seuil, Paris, 1942. Published under the pen name of Henri Davenson.

of the cultural heritage not only of the West but of the whole of humanity.

But I no longer wish to interpose a borrowed authority between the reader and this attempt at a simple meditation on the second request of the Our Father: "Thy Kingdom come." (I wonder if we realize what these words, so often repeated, really mean. When you stop to think about it they are so strange, especially in the clumsy artificiality of the vernacular translation. And, as we shall see, they have given rise to so many misinterpretations.) I, who am writing this, am simply a Christian with no special mandate, inquiring into the content of my faith. "Christian" is a difficult title to bear. Even Ignatius of Antioch, a saint who knew that he was on his way to martyrdom, asked for prayers so that he would show himself a true Christian, saying, "I want not merely to be called a Christian but actually to be one." (Letter to the Romans, 3:2.) So I must ask my reader not to be misled by the oratorical tone that this discourse takes (after all we have to use a little rhetoric from time to time; otherwise how can we express ourselves in public?). I have no intention of usurping the title of doctor or apostle; St. Augustine never wastes an opportunity of reminding us, "it is in vain that we preach the word of God without, if we do not begin by listening to it within." (Sermon 179, 1.)

And surely the first task for all of us is to rediscover the true meaning of the Christianity that we claim to profess in order to take on anew its full wealth of content and implications. Even on the level of faith, the problem is to *be* in truth and not just to appear to be. Such an effort to grow in a deeper awareness is especially important for those of us who live in a cultural setting that has been almost entirely dechristianized. So we can see the urgent need to react against a popular mentality, an attitude that has become so widespread, and nourish our thought and our action on the solid food of authentic Christian inspiration. This is already an indication of the orientation that this meditation will take. I am not concerned with elaborating a new treatise of apologetics: before we try to convert others, which is always very easy at least on paper, we have to work at our own conversion, and this has to be done in the first place on the doctrinal level. We have to inquire of ourselves what is the meaning of our profession of faith and see if, and how, it can shed light on the path we follow and guide our steps through the thick and shadowy jungle of History.

I must be forgiven for capitalizing the word. My intention is to make it clear that I am not dealing with the history that historians deal with, history as a science (defined as mankind's past insofar as documents exist that make it possible for us to know it). I am dealing with the problem of the history really lived by humanity throughout the whole of its duration and with which each one of us is intimately associated simply by the fact that our own existence is historical. In other words I am dealing with the problem of the "meaning of history." What is the meaning of that long march through the temporal dimension (I was going to write, this long pilgrimage, but I do not want to impose an Augustinian vocabulary on the reader from the very beginning)? What is the meaning of the long succession of empires, as the ancients would say; of civilizations, as we say today; of cultures, to adopt the German-American jargon of the ethnologists?

For the sake of subtle minds who judge it old-fashioned to state the problem in these terms and who question the very notion of "meaning," I would like to say that this word evokes an image rather than a concept, and that this image is twofold, borrowed on the one hand from the realm of mathematics and on the other from the field of semantics. Is history moving in one direction? Is it moving toward a goal? Is there any significance, any reason that can be understood by men, any value that can justify the expending of so much energy, so much suffering and bloodshed, that can explain so many great exploits and so many apparent reverses?

Men who were born to self-awareness and the life of the spirit immediately after the butchery of the First World War have always been haunted and devoured by anxiety over the great question raised by the history we have to live: what is the meaning of history? Our parents had known a time when the value of the franc, for example, unchanging for more than a hundred years, was linked by a chain of definitions to the dimensions of the world and, thence, to the cosmic system (a franc, five grammes of minted silver; the gramme, one cubic centimeter of distilled water; the meter, a ten-millionth of the quarter of the earth's circumference . . .) They clung to hope. They attempted to shut out the experience of the war as though it were simply a horrible parenthesis in the history of mankind. But we never believed this, and our first excursions into books only confirmed what our instinct told us ("we civilizations, we know now that we are mortal"). We have always known that the events of that horrible war had forever dispelled an illusion —a comfortable and ingenuous belief in a linear, continuous progress which vindicated Western civilization as the last stage of evolution reached by humanity. Our history texts quite frankly laid claim to this without in the least realizing the challenge that it posed. Ten years later, in 1929, came the financial collapse of Wall Street: the great economic crisis in which it seemed that capitalism would founder and sink and which confirmed our view that the world in which we lived was a broken world.

Is there any need to call to mind all the rest? The Russian Revolution which had taken place in the meantime with all its attendant convulsions (today, watching the progress of the race to the moon, it is easy to forget the price that was paid: civil war, famine, pitiless destruction and tyranny): the armed vigil of the thirties, fascism, the collective madness of the great, civilized nations. The peril was rising to a new level. Our childhood had been spent during the "Great War." At that time no one could foresee that it would be the first of a series. But our generation has lived through the horrors of a second World War, the Cold War, the revolutions of the Third World, the colonial wars.

Napalm has taken over where mustard-gas left off; guerilla warfare is taking the place, in many instances, of conventional warfare (oh, the euphemistic prudery of our vocabulary!); keeping the peace, when at all possible, amounts to no more than maintaining a balance of terror with the threat of atomic destruction always hanging over us.

Surely everyone who has lived through these tragic years has had the experience, on a day that has dawned more tragically than others, of seeing the dark, apocalyptic night pierced by a flash of lightning that has revealed the radical contingency of this earthly city. Augustine's contemporaries had the same vision when Rome was sacked by the Visigoths, and for all who have experienced it, it is a vision of unique and lasting value. It is up to us, to those of us who have had this vision, to remind the world of it when things appear to settle down again and go well with ourselves and those around us. It is up to us to look into it more closely and to draw the lesson from it.

There is a deeply felt need, all around us, to understand more about this mysterious process that bears us along so irresistibly. And this is also why there are so many diverse and often contradictory replies being formulated in the ideological Tower of Babel which is today's world. Like the length of women's skirts, which changes from one year to the next, a tyrannical fashion imposes doctrines on us. At the present moment the prevalent fashion is to disqualify all history. Anti-history is in vogue. Twenty years ago a lyrical philosophy of the absurd had captivated the attention of young people, the philosophy that is so well summed up in the bitter words of Macbeth: "Life's but a walking shadow, a poor player that struts and frets his hour upon the stage and then is heard no more: it is a tale told by an idiot, full of sound and fury, signifying nothing." In the meantime, at the other extreme of the doctrinal scale we have had to give battle to other dogmatic philosophies, so certain of possessing the secrets of history in its totality as well as in the present. In the name of this understanding of history we have seen these philosophies liquidate adversaries, antagonists and deviationists with implacable severity. No tyrant has ever been more absolute, no executioner more cruel than in those countries where men have believed themselves to be authorized interpreters and agents of destiny. (I use this word deliberately: the humanist would have a lot to say about the metamorphosis of the ancient notion of *Eimarmene.*)

But the most urgent duty of a Christian is not to make an inventory of these doctrines, which have been alternately rivals and allies. The first thing is to see whether the faith he professes sheds some light on the question. That is precisely our goal: to sketch a Christian theology of history, or rather, to help our reader to rediscover it for himself. In a sense such a theology is something new. It is the fruit of the many studies undertaken on this subject over a period of thirty years. And it is like the gospel story about the scribe who becomes a disciple of the kingdom of heaven: "he is like a householder who brings out from his storeroom things both old and new." The newest pages of our theology are often very ancient pages which have been neglected and forgotten for a long time and have been found again in their original freshness and lasting value only after long and arduous search.

2. *OUTMODED INDIVIDUALISM*

There is no real reason to be surprised at this. The history of Christian thought and the life of the Church are marked throughout their development by such rediscoveries and deeper penetration of ancient truths. This is all part of the phenomenon of rebirth so characteristic of the history of culture we see developing in an ebb and flow, a withdrawal and return—to borrow the language of Vico or Toynbee. In passing let me point out that this, in itself, is enough to demonstrate the inadequacy of a simplistic conception of progress.

But someone who takes his place within the Christian tradition should, before he goes any further, try to find out why a truth that he has just rediscovered with joy was neglected and hidden so long. He must shun the temptation to doctrinal opportunism. That an authentic theology of history fell into almost total neglect can be readily explained, it seems to me, once one recognizes this development as a corollary to the religious individualism, which was such an ingrained characteristic of Christianity as lived and perceived in Western societies in the course of the generations, indeed, the centuries which preceded us. That more or less radical individualism now appears to us a serious deviation from the authentic Christian message on the level of its practical consequences as well as on the doctrinal level.

This attitude has been so thoroughly corrected in our days that it now takes some effort of the imagination to understand its full import and attendant danger. It will be difficult for my younger readers to have any idea of the innovative, the almost revolutionary, character of Father Henri de Lubac's first major work, in 1938, *Catholicisme, les aspects sociaux du dogme* (Catholicism: The Social Aspects of Dogma). The ambiguous grandeur of the title served to make the novelty of the subtitle and the subject-matter acceptable. But we had to wait until the final version of the Constitution *Lumen Gentium* before the Second Vatican Council openly proclaimed the fundamental idea that, in the economy of salvation, the central place belongs to the notion of the Church as a community, as the "messianic people" of the New Covenant: "It has pleased God to make men holy and save them not merely as individuals without any mutual bonds, but by making them into a single people, a people which acknowledges Him in truth and serves Him in holiness . . . making them one, not according to the flesh but the Spirit." (Chap. 2, para. 9)

One could add many an anecdote to Father de Lubac's Introduction in which he portrays (the image barely distorted by being reflected in the mirror of an adversary) the "pure and strict individualism" (Hamelin) which was mistaken for the very essence of Christianity, in which man, alone with his God, could walk through "an invisible battle" (Charles Morgan), "a rose in his hand" (Giono). One only has to remember the hymn popular in France for so long: *I only have one soul to save!* I can still hear a philosophy professor who tried to impress upon us when we were twenty years old that, in contrast to Christian spirituality, the spirituality of the Old Testament always involved a concern for community since the psalm that begins with a personal cry of distress, *"From the depths I call to you, Yahweh,"* concludes with an expression of the hope of collective redemption for the people of God, *"it is he who redeems Israel from all their sins"* (Ps. 130).

This onesided emphasis on the destiny of the individual had its roots in the distant past. We can already see an exaggeration, almost an exclusiveness, in the phrase that Pascal puts into Jesus' mouth in his *The Mystery of Jesus:* "I thought of you in my agony; I poured out certain drops of blood for you." But as everyone knows, the Jansenist problem was itself a by-product of the Pelagian quarrel and in particular of the fact that, most regrettably, St. Augustine as he grew old, thought he could use the weapons chosen by his adversaries. It is unnecessary to stress how this initial option has led theology into some inextricable complications, concerning, for example, the problem of personal predestination considered in isolation from that of "the whole Christ."

But to come back to the matter at hand, it is quite obvious that by laying too much stress on the whole problem of personal salvation men were necessarily led to dissolve the problem of history which became, simply, the sum of individual destinies. Personal history also tended to shrink into insignificance by the same process. One only has to think of the almost complete obliteration of any sense of collective responsibility in those weird "examinations of conscience," concerned exclusively with the trifing problems of individual morality without ever emphasizing the much graver ones posed by economic and political life.

Of course we must take care not to exaggerate in the opposite direction today. In fact it is probably not too early to proclaim most emphatically that it is not a question of denying the autonomy of the human person. We must recognize that each man has some of the attributes of the monad, each man is certainly the object of a singular love on the part of his creator, that Absolute who is, himself, a personal being. Each man is, as it were, at the end of one particular ray of light flowing from the Sun of Justice and in this sense the caricature of the Christian who has a direct line to his God is not entirely based on error.

But when we look at it from another angle we also must recognize and firmly profess that the human condition—and the Christian condition is no exception—is a collective condition. We live a *social life* as St. Augustine was fond of emphasizing, going back to Aristotle's idea of the *"political life,"* developed by the Stoic philosophers (*City of God*, XIX, 5). By every fiber of his being man is attached to the historical community of which he is a part, to the city which gives him life, to the civilization which nourishes and gives form to his personal life. Whether he is conscious of it or not he has a share and a role of his own in their history. Here it is a question of history only in the most obvious and, as we shall see, in the most superficial meaning of the word. For each human person also has his role to play in another history, in the spiritual history, the economy by which the plan that God has chosen for the salvation of the world (*Heilsgeschichte*) is accomplished. This is the history that advances mysteriously toward the last day, the end of the world, in the twofold sense of ending and fulfillment.

3. THE ATROPHY OF ESCHATOLOGY

As the visible participation of each man in history comes to an end at the hour of his death, it is significant that the individualistic distortion of the Christian ideal was accompanied by a withering away of eschatological hope. People spoke of "the end of the world" which, in itself, is a very questionable expression. Even if it is true that "the world as we know it is passing away" (I Cor 7:31), as Augustine pointed out, it is the exterior form of this world that is disappearing, not the substance, "the figure, therefore, passes away, not the nature" (*City of God*, XX, 14). At the eschaton the cosmos will undergo a marvelous transformation and will be "renewed to some better thing" (*City of God*, XX, 16). But in men's minds the image of the last day was the image of calamity, desolation and terror which

the ancient prophets had depicted for the Day of Yahweh (Zp
1:15; Am 5:18). And, as it is expressed in the *Dies Irae*, people
were principally concerned with the individual day of judgment for
all sinful men: "Even the just will barely be saved." As though the
Day of the Lord's Coming were not also an object of hope! As
though Christians should not live in the joyful expectation of the
triumphant coming of Christ, who will "save us from the retribu-
tion which is coming" (1, Th 1:10). "Come, Lord Jesus" (Rv 22:
20). But at that time no one stopped to think about the *Marana tha*
(1 Co 16:22; Didache 10:6), and when the critics—A. Schweitzer
and, in France, A. Loisy—saw fit to emphasize the important part
played in the life of the early Christians by their impatient expectation of the Parousia, an illustrious theologian retorted sarcastically
that he had never known a Christian who found any serious nourishment for his spiritual life in this expectation!

G. Jossa has clearly shown[1] that there is an almost inevitable and
necessary link between a weakening sense of the theological meaning of history and a unilateral insistence on the problem of personal
sanctification. Even within Judaism this could already be seen in the
Wisdom literature insofar as it manifested a strain that ran counter
to the apocalyptic literature. In the period of its fullest development,
during the Hellenistic and Roman period, we can see the same
concern with self, the same withdrawal into the interior life. All
relationship with God seems to be considered as a purely individual
thing and, by the same token, messianic hope grows weaker until it
entirely disappears. Take the *Book of Wisdom* (Philo's work, except
for a few minor points, lays itself open to similar remarks): a sense
of history is not entirely absent, in fact it fills the whole of the
second part of the work (chapters 10 to 19), but this long meditation
on Israel's past breaks down into a series of examples, ranging from
Abel to Exodus, which are quoted to show that God is merciful to
the just and that he punishes the wicked. This is not history in the

[1] G. Jossa, *La Teologia della Storia nel Pensiere cristiano del secondo
Secolo*, Naples, 1965.

sense in which we use the word which implies unity, continuity and direction. There are practically no openings into the future, or only very vague ones; no direct allusion to the awaited Messiah. The only problem dealt with is that of wisdom and personal salvation.

This is a very widespread phenomenon. The awareness of taking part in the great collective adventure we call history fades from men's minds and is overshadowed by the strictly personal dramas, enacted in so many different situations, which cannot in themselves, be decisive, since the reactions they elicit are so various. It can happen to minorities rejected from the mainstream of the life of their time who withdraw, subjugated and powerless, within the walls of the ghetto. But the ghetto can also be a center of messianic ferment as is proved conclusively by the history of Judaism throughout the centuries, from the Babylonian Captivity and the Prophetic activity during that period evoked by Ezekiel and chapters 40 to 55 of Isaiah, all the way to modern times and the mystical circles so vividly described by Gershom Scholem. An extraordinary example would be Sabbatai Zevi (1625–1676), the apostate-Messiah of the Turkish Empire who, although he became a Muslim, continued to be venerated by his followers as though his apostasy concealed some mystery, and his prophet Nathan of Gaza, who was his John the Baptist and his Paul. On the other hand it can also happen within a flourishing civilization during a period of peace and security, especially to those who belong to the ruling classes of that society and benefit from the social system and the prosperity. Then the feeling grows that there is no more really historic work to be done. Was not this the case in our own civilization until very recently? "God's in his heaven, all's right with the world." Everyone simply has to cultivate his own private garden. This, in turn, leads us to the singular experience, characteristic of a major catastrophe, when the blood of innocents and martyrs cries aloud to heaven: "How long? . . ." The walls that enclose personal life are rent asunder, and in the brotherhood of a common destitution, as in the exaltation of a common struggle for survival, men rediscover that they are all bound together in a vast and immensely meaningful undertaking.

At this point they cannot but ask themselves: does history have meaning?

4. TRUE HISTORY

I have no intention of indulging in a tone of facile enthusiasm. On the contrary, I wish to speak in strictly reasonable terms. As the Apologists of the second century liked to say: "I am not speaking of things that are strange to me, nor is my undertaking unreasonable" (*Epistle to Diognetus* 11:1). The point is simply that Christians must become aware of the implications of their faith by entering more deeply its inner dimension. But this supposes a complete conversion of the mind. In this respect as in every other, Christianity demands that we undergo a radical and continual "conversion." "Repent" is the first word used by both John the Baptist (Mt. 3:2) and Jesus himself (Mt 4:17) in their public preaching and by Peter on the day of Pentecost (Ac 2:38). It is a key word that is as important as the "fear not" that recurs so constantly all through the Gospel. Both express the assurance that there is a solution and that that solution is a source of happiness. If we are capable of weaning ourselves from a narrowly earthbound point of view and from the false philosophies of the world around us, and of beginning to look at history with eyes that are specifically Christian, then we shall find that the reply to our question is already there, within our reach.

This rectification of our point of view is an elementary step to take, but it is also a decisive one. Before we can take it, however, we must consider on what level of being true history, the history that has meaning, is taking place. This is the crux of the matter, and it is the point at which it is both most difficult and most necessary to begin to free ourselves from habits of thought contracted in any given cultural environment that is "profane" and also profaned.

Instead of thinking of all history in relation to Christianity, we often judge Christianity and condemn or exalt it according to the civilizing or destructive role it has played in the domain of purely earthly realities. Where, indeed, is true history? It is obviously not that which we see with our eyes, or which is recorded in our chronologies —Olympiads, Consular Annals, Millennia. It is not empirical history that an historian seeks to reconstruct.

As far as that history goes, a Christian knows no more than any other—which is very little. Knowledge is astonishingly limited and fragmentary. There are, of course, philosophers who pretend to know much more about it, but the professional historian leaves them to their dreams and their arrogance. He himself is satisfied if, with some degree of assurance, he is able to cast a narrow ray of light on some small area of what can be known. His technical skill in no way frees him from the common condition of mankind. In spite of all our efforts, man's progress through time, seen in its totality, seems to our anxious eyes lost in darkness like an ocean in the night. We feel as though we were standing in the prow of a ship, looking out into the darkness ahead. We plunge forward, but the only sign of progress is the few yards of white foam we can see on the surface of the dark water. Historical science makes it possible for us to know and understand a certain number of things: the factors that motivated the Peloponnesian Wars, the evolution of conditions whereby slavery was transformed into serfdom, the rise and development of capitalism, the failure of European colonialism in the nineteenth century and other events of the same order, always limited in time and space. But once we have gathered up the threads of these different episodes of the human adventure we are no nearer to seeing order and direction in the way they follow each other, any more than we can see order in the irrational pattern of the stars scattered in the heavens.

I have to remind you that I am speaking as a professional historian, and I cannot disregard the experience I have gained in the exercise of my art. As I have said elsewhere,[2] the foremost lesson that is to

[2] H. I. Marrou, *De la connaissance historique*, Paris, Seuil, (collection Esprit) 5th Ed., 1966, p. 58.

be learned from every conscientious attempt to seek out, rethink and reanimate the past is one of humility. Every step of his way the historian is conscious of the immense learning he needs for his work but which is unattainable simply because of his human condition. Only a god, only God himself, can ever know, in all truth and in all its fullness, the whole of human history.

The little that our science does allow us to grasp gives us a glimpse of the structure of history and reveals it, in its concrete reality, as a structure of such complexity that the human mind can never hope to exhaust all its ramifications or grasp and define all its infinitely subtle interactions. History is never simple. Only by means of ruthless selectivity and arbitrary simplifications, which cannot be justified except as pedagogical method, can the historical theorist organize all the elements of any one period or civilization into an idea or a system. We can see an instance of this in the Middle Ages in the West, which has been popularly equated with Christendom itself, and yet so many currents of thought and so many different elements remained absolutely foreign and even hostile to the Christian faith during this period.

There are so many paradoxes, so many unexpected after effects, so many ruses of human reason. The most perfectly conceived laws are often applied in contradiction to their real purpose, institutions turn against those whom they were supposed to serve. An example of this can be seen in Roman Africa: Hadrian's noble law provided very liberally for a right of user which made the peasants quasi-proprietors of the land they cleared for cultivation in the vast imperial territories; hardly fifty years later, in the time of Commodus, the whole system tightened its grip on the peasants and turned against those who were supposed to have benefited from it, and the colonizers gradually became serfs.

I cannot help being reminded of the image so dear to Buddhist wisdom: every act of man is like a pebble thrown into a calm pond, and the ripples that it sets in motion reach out to infinity. To give a serious answer to the question, what is the meaning of history?, we would have to be able to take in the totality of everything that is happening, has happened, or will ever happen. Indeed, we would have to be God, the One "who is, who was, and who is to come" (Rv 1:4), and the historian is not God. He is a humble laborer who reminds his brothers that it is only given us to think as mortals. This is why he has such a deep, visceral repugnance for all the attempts that have been made in the West within the last two centuries to elaborate a philosophy of history.

And now it is the turn of the Christian to take over from the historian and to emphasize that these so-called philosophies are no more than poor imitations of theology. They only offer fallacious answers to a question that has been wrongly presented. They have sought to discover and to demonstrate the meaning of history, but their scope includes only earthly history. They consider history only insofar as it can be seen and grasped on the level of our experience. And what makes us so sure that the little that we can grasp of men's gestures does actually have any meaning?

5. PROFANED THEOLOGY

It has become commonplace to remark that this very notion of a philosophy of history in the cultural tradition of the West was inherited, or rather plundered from, Christian dogma. It is no accident that today's Westerner envisages the history of humanity with optimism, seeing it as analogous to evolution, a gradual creation, the slow building up of a superior form of being, an on-going development and improvement on the level of being. The fact is that this twofold notion of continuity and progress is simply the residue of a secularized form of the Judeo-Christian theology of history first introduced into the world of the Mediterranean basin by the Book of Daniel and gradually developed during the early centuries of our times in Patristic thought until it reached its fullest and most magnificent expression in the twenty-two books of the *City of God*.

This was a complex process, and we shall have to examine it a little more closely in order to put our finger on the exact spot at which our own attempt to readjust our point of view should be situated. As Raymond Aron[3] has shown so clearly, the philosophy of history current today is not simply and solely a transposition of our theology. In the first place there is not just one philosophy of history, a whole series exists in dialectical relationship with each other. As we all know, Marxism takes a stand in opposition to Hegel, whose philosophy it sets out to "reverse" in the most metaphorical sense of the word. But Hegel had set himself up in opposition to Kant, who in turn had so severely criticized the ideas of Herder. Herder himself, in his first essay, *Auch eine Philosophie der Geschichte,* published in 1774, was well aware that he was proposing a philosophy of history altogether different from that elaborated by the French philosophers of the Enlightenment (Turgot and Voltaire; Condorcet was not yet included in their ranks).

The deliberate intention of these philosophers was to make the transposition from the sacred to the profane, from theology to philosophy (even the choice of this term in their writings was not devoid of polemical intent). But the Christian thought which they rejected and opposed was itself not entirely uncontaminated by the world. It was Bossuet rather than Pascal who was the adversary of the philosophy of the Enlightenment. It was he who thought he could understand, in the light of Holy Scripture and of a very inept reading of the *City of God,* the meaning of the succession of empires, the significance of the history that is visible to the eyes of an historian. This was what he intended in his *Discourse on Universal History* and his *Politics.* Bossuet knew why Islam existed, why the English revolution had taken place!

In this respect he simply showed himself to be the heir of medieval tradition. The fundamental error in his interpretation of Augustine's teaching—that of taking Christendom to be synonymous with the City of God—had already been explicitly formulated, in all good faith, by the Bavarian Cistercian, Otto de Freising, uncle of Frederick

[3] Raymond Aron, *Dimensions de la conscience historique,* Paris, 1961, p. 34–36.

Barbarossa, around 1143–1146. He had modeled his *Chronicon* on
the Augustinian schema as a history of two cities, but when he
reached Book V and began to deal with the rise of the Christian
Empire he suddenly realized that "since everyone including, with
only a few exceptions, the Emperors themselves, had become devout
Catholics, it seems to me that I have written, not a history of two
cities but, to all intents and purposes, that of only one which I shall
call the Church . . ."[4] The confusion can be traced, even further
back, though. It existed in the time of Charlemagne and, even
before, in the time of the Visigoth Kings of Toledo. I will not
say, as it has now become fashionable to say, that the confusion has existed since the time of Constantine (in any case it
would be more exact to say, since Constans II and Theodosius) for,
seen from the perspective of Byzantium, the problem is far more
complex. To understand the ideal type of Western Christendom one
must take into consideration the somewhat simplistic barbarism of its
origins.

But this is not our present problem. The precise error that we set
out to pinpoint and denounce in the hope that it will lead to a rectification of our point of view was the error that was made in identi-
fying the construction and development of the Christian city and,
more particularly, within this, the growth of the spiritual society
which is the Church, with the construction and development of the
City of God, which is normally almost wholly hidden. It is not so
much for their plan to build a Christian city that the men of the
Middle Ages should be blamed as for the fact that they mistook
the means for the end or, to put it more precisely, for the fact that
they mistook the subordinate end for the supreme end; they con-
fused being-by-participation with its essential antitype; the figure,
shadow and image with the fundamental and ultimate reality.
Dilthey saw this very clearly with regard to Bossuet[5]: a principle

[4] Otto de Freising, *Chronicon*, in Hofmeister (V, Prol. p. 58).
[5] Dilthey, *Einleitung in die Geisteswissenschaften*, 1883, French Translation 1942, p. 128–129.

of secularization was involved by which the absolute was projected into the relative, the transcendental into the empiric.

A mutilated and thereby desecrated view of history had gradually been accepted as quite natural by Christian thought. And the day that a dechristianized philosophy appeared and detached this view of the world from its supernatural context the inevitable outcome was that history was seen as an entity sufficient unto itself simply on the level of humanity empirically observable. This is just what happened with the appearance of the philosophy of the eighteenth century.

As we can now see, we have to revise a position which goes back a long way in time. We not only have to rid ourselves of the deceptive prestige of the neo-pagan ideologies in the world around us, we also have to correct our sights and adjust our course within the Christian tradition. We have to go back a long way, all the way to the source and principle, to the glowing core at the heart of our faith. At the outset of our reflection we must posit that God exists (nothing is more beautiful or more noble to contemplate than the fact that God is) and that we know he is there, sustaining all beings, the Lord of history. He not only makes it possible for us to know history; everything that happens in history happens because he has willed or permitted it. He has taught us to call on him as Father: this is the first foundation of our assurance and of our trust in history, our faith in his providence and love. We know that the unfolding of the ages since the first day of creation is in his all-powerful and merciful hand.

Even when evil enshrouds the world and seems to gain the upper hand, when cosmic catastrophes blow us about like chaff in the wind, we must not despair. God has loved men so much that he has sent his only Son to save them (Jn 3:16) and "we know that by turning everything to their good, God co-operates with all those who love him, with all those that he has called according to his purpose . . . to become true images of his Son . . ." (Rm. 8:28–29). When history takes on its most sinister aspect and seems to us to be simply the theater of suffering, unhappiness, failure and death, then we must remember that Scripture has given a solemn promise, reiterated three different times, that the day will come when "the Lord Yahweh will wipe away the tears from every cheek" (the verse of Is 25:8 is repeated twice in the Book of Revelation, 7:17 and 21:4). Even if it never taught us anything else about history, even if history were destined to remain completely obscure and incomprehensible to us, our faith in his love should be enough to make us capable of living through the ordeal of time without blasphemy in spite of the inevitable heartbreaks.

6. THE TRIPTYCH OF HISTORY

However we have not been left with such a crude, unsubtle faith. Revelation has been given and has taught us about the mystery of the divine plan, the economy of salvation. And here we can put our finger on the deepest paradox of the Christian faith: just when we are in danger of being crushed by the realization of our unworthiness, we can proclaim with pride that it has been given to man to know something of the unfathomable purpose of God.

It is one of the characteristics of the Christian religion that it does not restrict itself to truths that concern the eternal being or beings-by-participation. It is true that our profession of faith begins by confessing God who is One and Trinity and then God the Creator, but alongside this teaching about God in himself ("theology" properly so-called, to use the expression of the Greek Fathers) there is also a teaching concerning the "economy," the divine plan for salvation, the intervention of God the Savior within sinful humanity, within the temporal dimension of history. We only have to open the letters of St. Paul: at almost every page we can see his unbounded enthusiasm at having been charged by God to reveal "the message which was a mystery hidden for generations and centuries," "kept secret for endless ages," "which has now been revealed to his saints," and which must be "broadcast to pagans everywhere" (Col 1:26; Rm 16:25–26; see also I Co 2:7, 10). God is the Lord of history and of the cosmos. As the Prophet Daniel put it: "His to control the procession of times and seasons, to make and unmake kings" (Dn 2:21). And we should also remember the very carefully worded phrases of St. Paul in his speech before the Council of the Areopagus: "From one single stock he not only created the whole human race so that they could occupy the entire earth, but he decreed how long each nation should flourish and what the boundaries of its territory should be. And he did this *so that all nations might seek the deity* and, by feeling their way towards him, succeed in finding him" (Ac 17:26–27). It was so that they would succeed in finding him that he who proclaimed himself to be the Way, the Truth and the Life, took human flesh and became man (Jn 14:6). And so this is how the secret of history was revealed to us, "He has let us know the mystery of his purpose, the hidden plan he so kindly made in Christ from the beginning to act upon when the times had run their course to the end: that he would bring everything together under Christ, as head" (Ep 1:9–10).

So there it is! If God has placed men on the earth, if he has said to them "increase and multiply"—the fundamental blessing that even sin could not destroy, as Augustine, that so-called pessimist, likes to point out (*City of God* XXII, 24, 1)—this does not mean that his destiny lies within the limits of his earthly life: men are not on earth in order to evolve from the stone age to the age of the atomic bomb; they are there in order "to seek the deity by feeling their way towards him." And as not only the Athenians but the whole of humanity has gone astray in that quest and has failed to find him, the Father, in his overflowing mercy and his eternal wisdom, has established this "economy," this temporal "dispensation," which once again makes it possible for us to reach him. Man is not on earth simply to build up empires and civilizations but in order to unite himself to Christ, to become incorporated with him, to be saved, sanctified and deified by him and in him.

We do not need to worry any more: now we know. We know why we have received the gift of life, of movement and of being; we know where we are going. We know where all men are going—I decline to use the word "humanity," it has been so completely emptied of all real meaning for us; it needs to be reinvested with the full value of the real and not just the generic unity, the concrete substance, that it had for the early Fathers, particularly for Gregory of Nyssa.

This is the truth that has been revealed to us. This is the point from which we can start and to which we must constantly refer to take our bearings. In the time of St. Thomas (and even before, with Synesius of Cyrene) human reason faced a dilemma: in order to deny the Aristotelian idea of the eternity of the world they had to call upon their knowledge of revelation to affirm that time had a beginning. Today it is not so much an affirmation as a question that is the stumbling block for men. A Christian, relying on God's word, declares himself to be the unworthy bearer of the answer to the question. This answer is good news: Yes, history does have meaning, value and relevance. It is a history of salvation.

In the light of revelation we can picture the history of mankind as a vast triptych. In the center is the Incarnation, the eternal Word made man for us and for our salvation, his kenosis, his humility and humiliation, his obedience "unto death" on the cross of Calvary —which is at the very heart and center of our faith—and, inseparably part of this, the glorious resurrection, first-fruits and guarantee of another resurrection. This central phase of history is very brief chronologically speaking, only a few years—"When he started to teach, Jesus was about thirty years old," Luke 3:23 and his public life only lasted a number of months. And yet in itself it fills the whole of the main panel of the triptych, and we should prefer it above all others, coming back to it constantly in meditation, for the mystery of the Incarnation contains the essence of all reality. In it all the tangled threads of history are unravelled and woven into a harmonious whole.

However, we should not be in too much of a hurry to push aside the two panels that flank the central picture. Even if their importance is secondary to that of the central panel, they are still important in the architecture of the whole structure. On the left-hand panel can be seen the long unfolding of the centuries before the coming of Christ, the Old Testament times or, to be more exact, the period of gradual preparation for the Gospel in which God "prepared the human race, in many diverse ways, to be attuned to salvation" (Irenaeus, IV: 14, 2). The pagans are not excluded from the picture. From Justin Martyr to Eusebius and—to include modern scholars—Arnold Toynbee, so many men have been at pains to underline the fact that the *Logos,* the creative Word has never completely abandoned men to the powers of darkness. Very often "Homer prophesies without knowing it, Plato speaks as a disciple of the Word, the poets, too, are taught by the Spirit" (Clement of Alexandria, *Instructor,* I.36, 1; 82, 3; I.28, 2). However, it is true that the real substance of this first act is played out primarily in the history of the beloved, chosen people. After the promise made to Abraham, the faith of the Patriarchs, the Exodus and the Covenant of Sinai, the Law was given to Israel to guide it towards Christ, as the slave-tutor guides his master's child through the dangers of the streets to school (Ga 3:24). Through all their infidelities and their vicissitudes "Yahweh your God was training you as a man trains his child" (Dt 8:5); King David, Jerusalem, the teaching of the Prophets gradually becoming more and more spiritualized, the meager remnant of Israel brought home after the Exile, the growing impatience of those who awaited the coming of the Messiah. . . . The gradual education of the Jewish people is like the rich, heavy sap seeping upward in the trunk of a tree. In the stained glass of the great Gothic cathedrals we can see the tale: the offshoot of the stock of Jesse, of which the fruits are John, the last Precursor, and Mary, the pure servant in whom the Word became flesh.

I would like to pause here for a moment. Both in the sacred history of the first Covenant and, more generally, in the time of preparation for the Gospel that I have already mentioned, a common feature is present; and that is that the time of human history is indissolubly bound up with the fulfillment of the divine "economy" of salvation. As Christian theologians have never tired of repeating, the divine plan of salvation works itself out in time and by means of time. Time is charged with positive value: it is neither an illusion, like the mirage created by Maya in the Indian Veda, nor an emanation of evil as it is for a neo-Platonist (for example, Porphyry writes, in his letter to Marcella, of "the soul's fall into the state of flux," equivalent in his spirituality to our notion of original sin). No! Time is an attribute of creation, born together with creation and inseparably bound up with it and God has willed that time should be the vector of salvation, the medium for the realization of the *oikonomia*. At this point we are on solid ground, the rock on which our theology of history can be built.

And now, without further delay, we must look at the third panel of the triptych, for it is still present and represents the third act of the drama of human history, the third and final phase of God's plan. It has its own special role to play in the economy of salvation just as the pre-Christian times and the time of the first Covenant. As we have said, it is, of course, the central panel that contains all that is essential. One might almost say that, measured against the yardstick of the Incarnation and Passion of the divine Word, any other event that might still occur would, in a certain sense, be insignificant, almost nonexistent. But our Lord was both God and man and we are only men. This is something that Christian thinking must never tire of repeating—for instance in the face of Indian thought in which the incarnation is simply one avatara amongst others. There is only one God and there is only one Son of God, the Only-Begotten (this title is used in the very earliest professions of faith and has constantly been solemnly reaffirmed by the Councils). He became man only once, he suffered once under Pontius Pilate, for all the sins of men, and salvation has been won, *once and for all* (Rm 6:10; Heb 7:27; 9:12; 10:10). Paul uses the phrase again and again.

7. THE TIME OF THE CHURCH

But we must be careful not to confuse different orders and levels of being and conclude that, since the decisive act has already been accomplished, nothing further of any importance can happen in history on the level of our lives as human beings. Something must still be going on since the triumphant return of Christ, the sign of the conclusion and consummation of the history of the world, has not yet come about, since the Lord has explicitly told us to pray for the coming of his kingdom. The triumph of the Ascension does not accomplish everything since it has not yet fulfilled "Yahweh's oracle to you, my Lord, 'Sit at my right hand and I will make your enemies a footstool for you.'" The "nations in uproar," the "kings on earth rising in revolt, princes plotting against Yahweh and his Anointed" must still be subdued. (I limit myself to quoting from the two greatest messianic Psalms, 2:1–2 and 110:1.) That the Parousia seems to be overdue, that there is a time of delay, has been a stumbling block for those who have believed in a "consequent eschatology." We should meditate upon this delay in the light of faith. However impatiently the first generation of Christians looked forward to the Parousia (can we really measure their impatience?), an attentive reading of the Gospel texts makes it clear that, however short it may be, the period between the two parousias was recognized as having a part to play in the history of salvation[6] It is evident that Jesus' teaching foresaw an intermediary time, a "time of the mission, a time of santification,"[7] a time of growth and progress, the time of the Church.

It is not my intention to attempt to reconstruct the story of how

[6] See the excellent study in O. Cullmann, *Salvation in History*, New York, Harper & Row, 1967.
[7] *Ibid.*

28

the early Church gradually became aware of the content of the revelation brought by Jesus or to go into the different stages in which the New Testament was written. It is an object of faith in its entirety, as it stands today: the four Gospels lie open before us and we only have to look at the teaching deriving from the parables of the kingdom to see the outlines of a picture of an interim period, the first approximation of a theology of the time of the Church.

In the first place this time is one of waiting. It is a time for being on the lookout for the return of the master of the house, the owner of the vineyard, the king who has gone to be crowned (Lk 19:13), the arrival of the bridegroom. This is the time for all the Lord's servants and handmaids, whether faithful or negligent, wise or foolish, to watch and wait. It is not a time of purely passive and submissive expectation. It is a time for work, for every man has been given the means (Mk 13:34) to accomplish his assigned task, whether as doorkeeper or as having a charge to distribute to his brothers their food in due season. This is the period in which the "talents," the capital entrusted to us, must be made to bear fruit, when we must be busy in the vineyard of the Lord whatever the hour at which we were hired—this in respect to the hour in history as well as to the hour in our own life. As the Church Fathers, and especially Augustine, have shown, these parables can be understood to refer to our personal lives as well as to the whole of human history.

The time of the Church is a time of mysterious growth, a slow maturing, as is suggested by the parable of the fig-tree whose branches become flexible and whose leaves unfold in the spring. For the kingdom of heaven is like the seed of the mustard plant, which is the smallest of all seeds but which sprouts and grows tall until it becomes like a tree in which birds can take shelter. Or again it is like a seed that a man has sown in the ground and which sends out shoots and grows, first as a leaf, then as an ear and finally as an ear heavy with ripe grain; and all this goes on night and day, whether the sower sleeps or wakes. The kingdom of God is also compared to a field, the field of the world, in which the good grain and the bad grow up side by side (we shall have to go into this more carefully later) and both are left standing until the time of the harvest. And finally it is compared to the little handful of leaven mixed deep into the dough, which raises up the whole batch so that it can be baked into loaves of bread.

By means of these images, in this semi-secret language, the New Testament gives us some idea of what the third panel of our triptych must represent. This can only be an approximation, for the picture is far from being finished. One whole section of the canvas is still untouched, whereas the history of the Old Testament could be laid out, if it were technically possible to do so, in all its details, like the old Flemish altar pieces that were so perfectly rendered down to the tiniest flower. The time of the church is now. History is not accomplished, and it is up to us, through our own endeavor and action, to contribute to the writing of it, and work toward its fulfillment.

I must not be accused of being a wicked Pelagian when I speak like this. I have simply attempted to interpret half a verse in Peter's letter in which he exhorts us not only to long for but also to *hasten* the parousia of the Day of the Lord (2 P 3:12). This is *our* time. The time that has been given to us to live, in which God has placed us and in which we have a task to fulfill, however, humble it may be. But the point is not so much to realize how important this task is, at the risk of exaggerating it. The point is to accomplish it. Let us hope that one day, like the servants in Luke (Lk 17:10), we shall be in a position to say "we have done no more than our duty." Finally this is the time during which our destiny is taking shape.

Once again I must stress that there is no question of attempting to balance or compare what we can do with what has already been accomplished, once and for all, on the cross at Calvary. But we have to drive out the demon of quietism which a unilateral stress upon the magnitude and the efficacy of the work that Christ has accomplished could lead to. Certainly salvation has already been won, but the moralist must transpose this truth onto his own register and say, simply, that salvation is offered to us. It is now up to us not to betray God's purpose for us, not to be unfaithful to the mission that he asks us to fulfill. It is true that we can say in unison with pagan wisdom "We are nothing more than men, weak and mortal beings," but our humility has a quite different ring to it: we recognize in fidelity and joy that this is the will of a God who is all love. This human condition is the condition that our Creator chose to assign to us, it is to this service that we have been called and not to another.

In other words, if God has willed that there should be an interval of time between the Ascension and the last day of the world, it cannot be his intention that this period between the two appearances of the Incarnate Word should be empty and pointless. Something is going on here, something that is necessary to the full realization of the divine plan of salvation. We cannot know how long, chronologically speaking, this interval, this third phase of history, will last. The Son of Man himself told us that, speaking as a man amongst men, he does not know it (Mt 24:36; Mk 13:32). We should understand from this that it cannot be revealed to us while we are still living in the human condition. We know, of course, that he will return like a thief in the night and that in that day the world will be as it was in the days of Noah and of Lot when, without a thought for what lay ahead, people ate and drank, took husband or wife (Mt 24:37), bought and sold, planted and built . . . (Lk 17:28). But even if it is not given to us to know the "times or dates that the Father has decided by his own authority" (Ac 1:7), still God has not left us in complete ignorance of what is going on in the hidden depths of history, in the history of this time, our history.

8. HOW LONG MUST WE WAIT

Revelation has told us very explicitly that we must open the book containing the secrets of history and of destiny. We can find this in the Book of Revelation, in the passage which tells of the breaking of the fifth seal. I would like to tell the prudent reader not to be astonished or disturbed about being referred to this most mysterious of all books. I can well understand his mistrust. The Book of Revelation has been used so often in the course of the Church's history to justify the wildest figments of the imagination! But I am not choosing this verse at random. It is a passage that ecclesiastical tradition has recognized as having special significance and that Christian reflection has often pondered with special affection. This is one of those cases in which we can speak of an interpretation resulting from "the unanimous consent of the Fathers," to quote the famous rule laid down by the Council of Trent and reiterated by the First Vatican Council (Denzinger, 995, 1788). This is not the time or place to examine at any length the different documents that constitute this extraordinary Patristic brief. It is enough to mention that it runs from Justin Martyr to Gregory the Great and includes Clement of Alexandria, Hippolytus of Rome, Tertullian and of course, as always, Origen, and that—to mention only the greatest and most important minds—Gregory of Nyssa, for the Eastern Fathers, is the counterpart of Augustine for the West. In the writings of the latter this text can be found ten times and in at least seven cases it is cited in relation to the theology of history.

And so, as humble members of the "taught Church," let us have the courage to follow the teaching of these Fathers and open the sacred book and read (Rv 6:9–11): "When he broke the fifth seal, I saw underneath the altar the souls of all the people who had been killed on account of the word of God, for witnessing to it. They shouted aloud, 'Holy, faithful Master, how much longer will you wait before you pass sentence and take vengeance for our death on the inhabitants of the earth?' Each of them was given a white robe, and they were told to be patient a little longer, until the roll was complete and their fellow-servants and brothers had been killed just as they had been."

As I have said, tradition has been unanimous on the subject. And it seems to me that even at a first reading the meaning is quite clear. The last verse means that history will come to a close, that it will have reached its end, having exhausted all its capacity for fecundity, only when the number of the martyrs—I would like to be bold and to generalize as the Fathers did and say: when the number of the saints—has reached its fullness. To be more exact, we might say: history will have reached its end when the last of the just has reached the zenith of his spiritual growth. The length of our history is the length of time that is necessary to fill up the ranks of the just, to build the City of God. All the Fathers are in agreement on this point: in questions concerning the essence of the faith, all the spiritual families, the different schools of theological thought, converge and agree. Every Christian who raises the problem, even if he is the lowliest of all the faithful, finds instinctively, within the heart of his faith, this same answer even without explicit reference to or memory of the text of Revelation and the approved commentaries. We need not be surprised, therefore, to learn that Father Sertillanges wrote in some notes on history that were published posthumously[8]: "Progress in Christianity is not linear and horizontal, it is vertical. It aims at eternity, not the spinning out of time. The reason for the existence of time is that we should move out of it, soul by soul. When the number of souls foreseen by the Lord has been reached, time will come to an end, whatever the condition of humanity may be at that moment. . . ."

Perhaps the modern reader feels very ill at ease with the notion of a "number that must be completed," especially if he is still obsessed by the memory of the too individualistic Christianity of the generations which preceded us, who were too exclusively focused on the distressing (and probably false) problem of predestination and of personal salvation. It is certainly very important not to have an atomized notion of history, as though it were nothing more than the summation of the host of individual souls, each of which has run the course of his own spiritual adventure.

But the collective aspect of history, which—quite rightly—seems to us today to be so important, must not make us forget the reality

[8] A. D. Sertillanges, *Pensées inédites, De la vie, De l'histoire,* Forcalquier, 1964, p. 119.

of the personal aspect: each one of us, in our irreducible singularity, is *also* one of the aspects of the humanity that Christ came to save. And the experience of the inner life makes it possible for us to understand better the way in which the drama is unfolding on the scale of the whole—the microcosm of our personal history reflects, in a certain sense, the macrocosm of collective history. Sometimes, on rare occasions, we can glimpse or conjecture that the Lord has prolonged the life of one of his servants in order to allow his spiritual maturation, or the work he is engaged in or the influence he exerts around him to reach a higher degree of perfection. This is the meaning of the vision that the holy monk, Apollonius of Hermoupolis, is said to have had and in which he heard the Lord say: "He still owes me a little time on earth in view of his own perfection and until he has been able to form an immense body of monks, imitators of his virtues." . . . (Hist. Monach. 8:17).

Once this point is conceded and seen in its proper perspective we are bound still to repeat that history must, nevertheless, be envisaged first and foremost in its totality and unity. "Jerusalem restored! The city, one united whole!" (Ps 122:3) The bad Latin of the Old Psalter (and I am not at all sure that the later translators have done any better) expresses quite clearly what is meant: the city of God is a whole—the image of a living body, as we shall see, is in no way arbitrary or misleading—a unity whose parts are interdependent. We must watch it growing, layer upon layer built of living stones. We are those living stones (I P 2:5), and we are building up the edifice that rises on the foundations laid by the Prophets and the Apostles (the metaphor of "edification," the construction of a building which has unfortunately been so debased, is very meaningful in itself for anyone who can recapture its original significance). Jesus Christ himself is the cornerstone, and the whole building is aligned on him and grows up into one holy temple in the Lord. Each one of us, with the whole of our personal history, is incorporated into this structure so that we may become, all together, one dwelling in which God lives, in the Spirit (Ep 2:20–22).

9. THE BODY OF CHRIST

This great gathering of the saints, of saved humanity, has its own name: the Church. At this juncture we shall not define the structure of the Church nor go into details about its boundaries. It is sufficient that we attempt to grasp its nature, its being. Speaking of the Church, the early Fathers used many images taken from one or other Testament, and the Second Vatican Council lists some of them (Lumen Gentium, 6): the sheepfold, the tract of land to be cultivated and, as we have seen, the edifice of God, the house (as one used to say, the king's household), the temple, the holy city, the bride. But the New Testament offers another image, used by St. Paul, to which tradition has given a higher place, not the building being constructed with living stones, but the body which grows as an organic whole. This is the body of Christ which is the Church (Ep 1:22; Col 1:18–24), the Body of which Christ is the Head and we are the members, the "fulness of him who fills the whole creation" (Ep 1:22). The better to stress the unity that embraces the Head and members, St. Augustine had the audacity to forge the richly significant expression "the whole Christ," which he used to speak of the whole that comprises both Head and members. I could mention more than two hundred instances in which the term is used: it recurs constantly in his preaching and especially in the *Enarrationes* on the Psalms. It must, of course, be clearly understood that the unity so strongly stressed here does not impair, in any way, the obvious subordination in which mankind, saved by Christ, stands in relation to Christ the Savior. The whole body receives strength and cohesion from the Head through the organic unity that binds them together (Col 2:19), and this is how it is able to grow with a divine growth until it becomes the perfect man, "fully mature with the fulness of Christ himself." (Ep. 4:13).

St. Augustine invites us to understand this verse, which exegetes today tend to apply to the more limited question of our own immediate and concrete problem of growth and sanctification, as applying to the collective growth of the Body of Christ—the Mystical Body, as modern theologians would say. Putting words into the mouth of Christ, Augustine imagines him addressing the Father: "and so, as the Saints come to be progressively gathered together in me, you will complete my Body, which has grown to its full perfection" (*Enarr. in Ps* 30, 1, 4).

And so the meaning of the period that follows after Christ is made manifest: human history continues even after the earthly life of the incarnate Word, the center and key of history, because time is necessary for the full growth of the mystical Body of Christ, and to complete the construction of the City of God. St. Paul sometimes joins the two images in one and speaks of "building up the Body of Christ" (Ep 4:12). History will come to an end when the work that has begun with the Incarnation is fully accomplished, thereby accomplishing the mystery of God's benevolent will to gather and recapitulate all things in Christ.

This is what has been explicitly spoken, revealed to us. This is certain. To be or become truly Christian we have to rediscover that fundamental truth: it is Christ's mystical Body that is the true subject of history, just as the full growth of this Body is the reason and the measure of the period of time which is still going on. The preconceived ideas fixed in our minds from our unconscious participation in a non-Christian civilization must be revised in relation to this certainty.

10. TRUE AND FALSE PROGRESS

Let us begin with the notion of progress. Before progress became the idol which today seems to oppose itself to our faith, the idea of progress was (and it still remains) a truth in the Christian order of things. But we must be sure to understand the subject of progress. What is it that advances and grows and, at each moment, is of a higher quality than it was the moment before? It is the Body of Christ, growing toward its full stature and perfection. Every generation and every century in turn bears its own fruits, represented by the cohort of saints who swell the ranks of those standing in the presence of the "triumphant Lamb," "the conqueror who will conquer yet again." It is the City of God that is gradually rising, as one course of stones is laid on another. Year by year and century by century, surely and steadily it comes closer to its accomplishment, which will bring history to an end.

To express his ideas about the members and the unity of this body St. Augustine developed the image of one man who, spread over the whole face of the earth, would go on growing throughout the centuries (see *Enarr.* in Ps 118, 16 and 6 etc. The image recurs frequently in his writings). The same image is used by Pascal in his *Fragment du Traité du vide:* "Thus in the course of so many centuries the whole succession of men must be regarded like a single individual who lives on and who is constantly learning." But Pascal applied this to the advance of science in Western civilization and not to the growth of the Church! This was an unjustified, and, frankly, an absurd, transposition!

Such a misinterpretation was the result of a slow degeneration which, as Etienne Gilson has shown, was already visible in the thirteenth century in the work of St. Bonaventure, for instance.[9] The notion of progress underwent a transposition from the realm of revealed truth and absolute certitude to the realm of hypothesis and a completely relative view of things. With a clear conscience Pascal spoke as a successor of Galileo at the time when classical physics was rising to its greatest heights. But he attached too little importance to the fragility of all civilizations, the phenomenon of decadence and the precariousness of all periods of renascence. Today we have a view of history that is more complex and, consequently,

[9] Etienne Gilson, *The Spirit of Mediaeval Philosophy* (Gifford Lectures 1931–1932), New York, Charles Scribner, 1936.

less optimistic. The past is no longer seen simply as the embryonic development of our own culture, it is also, and perhaps primarily, seen as the burial ground of civilizations that have disappeared and of cities that are lying in ruins.

One of the major examples of this, pre-Colombian America, will probably come immediately to the reader's mind: what is left of the creative will of the men who built such original monuments and, to mention only the experience of the Mayans, who had such a highly developed science of astronomy and mathematics that they calculated the length of the solar year with an error of less than twenty seconds. Can all these complicated structures have existed simply in order that corn, tomatoes and beans could be handed on to our modern economy? Or, to speak of the ruins that are closer to my own heart, what historian of classical Greece can fail to be most poignantly aware of the irreplaceable loss of the man of Greece just at that moment when he most clearly glimpsed his greatness?

But this misinterpretation is, above all, such a desecration! The privilege that belonged to the spiritual, religious and supernatural side of humanity has been credited to man himself as an earthly being.

The mention of these striking mis-readings of history will have given my reader some idea of the extent to which he is going to have to correct his way of thinking, the authentic conversion that he is going to have to undergo to rediscover an authentically Christian view of history. Also, after so many collective misadventures and catastrophes, it should no longer be necessary, it seems to me, to insist upon the mythical character of the notion of progress—that is, progress seen on the level of human life as it is lived within the limits of its earthly context—as it dominated Western thought from the Enlightenment to the Scientism of the nineteenth century. Men were simply intoxicated by progress in the scientific and technical domain, the gradual identification of human history with the biological evolution of the species, the confident extrapolation from experiments to conclusions that were only hoped for but which seemed inevitable. Men lingered with complacency over the good things that had been obtained but refused to recognize the evils which were the price that had been paid. It is true, there was an unprecedented progress in the technical area, but the price was an enslaved proletariat and a Third World exploited to the point of famine.

Even for those who benefited from technical progress there was a heavy price to pay! It is true that heavy industry and mass production brought better hygiene and greater material comfort within the reach of the new world aristocracy of "developed" nations, but a high price was demanded in return, the increasing banality of life! The disappearance of craftsmanship, the standardization of products and the horror of a civilization of housing projects: noise invading and destroying all silence, the growing agitation and the disappearance of quiet and contemplation. Science was growing and controlling the forces of nature, but the inner life of man atrophied in the process. Man was abandoned to his primary impulses, consciousness became more and more alienated, stupefied by the mass media. Today our immediate ancestors seem like the Sorcerer's apprentices who have let loose a wild and ungovernable process of which we are prisoners.

Let us take just one example: It was understood that the machine would liberate man from the servitude of having to supply his own needs, thereby making a reality of what Aristotle formulated as an unrealistic hypothesis: "If all our instruments, having received their orders or having the presentiment of what they should do, could accomplish their proper task like the legendary statues of Dedalus or the tripods of Hephaistos which, in the words of the poet, could automatically enter the assembly of the gods,—if the shuttles could weave by themselves, and the plectra play the zither, then the contractors would have no more need of workers nor the masters of slaves!"[10] Already, in several sectors of industrial production, we have reached the stage of automation. Workshops and factories function, as they say, "by themselves"; only one worker is needed to

[10] Politics, I, 4, 3, 1253 b34–1254 a1.

watch the various dials which show that the whole thing is working smoothly: "he lingers on as a machine-herd" wrote Lewis Mumford, optimistically, in 1934.[11]

This picture of bucolic "lingering" entirely disregards the nervous exhaustion that results from the unflagging attention these machines require. On the other hand, even discounting this human factor, can we really say, in the case of a power-station for instance, that the power is produced for us without the work of slaves, simply by the work of the hydraulic resources of the mountain and by automation? No, we cannot, for these wonderful machines have had to be designed and built, they are constantly in need of maintenance. Before long they need to be repaired (the telephone is there so that we can call for help), and they have hardly begun to pay for themselves when they have to be replaced.

There is no sign in society as a whole, even if we only consider the more technically advanced countries, that the development of machinery has really liberated man and set him free from the degrading work of a slave. In Aristotle's time there was at least one class that was fortunate, a group of free men who reaped the profits of the slave system and enjoyed the leisure it afforded them for culture and contemplation. Today, in the era of "executives," apart from a handful of playboys, there are no more masters. Everyone is a slave to the same alienating work, from the least important unskilled worker to the President and General Manager in danger of thrombosis.

For the sake of brevity I have decided to speak in terms of the past as though this illusion had completely disappeared from the popular mentality, and yet it still underlies much of our thinking. On the one hand it is obvious that ever since the Trilobites, biological evolution has taken place according to a law of progress. On the other hand, it is equally true that within the limits of a technical system the latest model of any product is superior to earlier attempts. The fraud consists in aligning these two experiences, which are of quite different

[11] Lewis Mumford, *Technics and Civilization,* caption to Plate XI, 1.

orders, and then deducing a would-be law of historical development from this. I am not speaking for the neo-scientists for whom the history of mankind is no more than the history of the development of our scientific technique and for whom, therefore, the different phases of the past are at best an instant in the embryonic development of the present or a divergent branch of evolution, and, therefore, useless.

It would be good to pause here for a moment to consider the notion of evolution. It is simply a theoretical model, curiously anthropocentric (or, to be more exact, built around the axis of *homo sapiens*), which has been elaborated for a very specific purpose: to explain the diversity and genesis of the different species. It cannot simply be transposed, as it stands, to a completely different level and used to explain the history of man—at least if, as Christian revelation invites us, we understand the history of man as implying the absolute value of the human person, of every human person ("the very hairs of your head are numbered"). We cannot resign ourselves to considering civilizations which may be marginal as far as our own direct line of development is concerned—to use the same example: the Mayan civilization—with the same detachment that we have with respect to the abortive branches of biological evolution such as the equidae of the American Tertiary period.

11. THE TWO CITIES

From our point of view we must again stress the fact that the ideology of progress transposed onto the level of earthly civilization implied an optimism that was not only ingenuous but also culpable for the complacency it fostered. The view of history that Christianity offers is more complex and more somber. It is significant that when St. Augustine tried to find an image which would be a synthesis of the whole unfolding of the human saga throughout all time, he found it was not sufficient simply to use that of an assured growth of the Body of Christ. He proposed a picture in two parts, in which the destiny of two rival cities seemed to be doing battle: "For this whole time of world-age, in which the dying give place and those who are born succeed, is the career of these two cities of which we treat" (*City of God* XV, 1). There is the City of God and then there is that other City which it is more difficult to define with one word. We should not be in too much of a hurry to call it the City of Satan. This term is favored by Tyconius rather than by Augustine, who uses it very rarely, and then only in a rhetorical manner. Satan, man's adversary, is not an "anti-God." To call it the "City of Evil" would not be accurate either, for evil is a deficiency in being. It is not a positive principle which could be the foundation for the construction of a City.

To be accurate, the City that is in conflict with the City of God is the Earthly City. However, in saying this we should immediately give a word of warning: this expression should not be understood as it is commonly meant today, to mean the best possible organization of our earthly dwelling. The Earthly City that Augustine speaks of is the human city, the too exclusively human city in which man, forgetful of his vocation for eternity, shuts himself up in his own finitude and takes what should be only a means or, at most a secondary goal subordinated to a higher goal, as the only goal and end of his action. It is the city in which man forgets God and becomes an idolater of himself. Need I remind you of the famous saying. "Two cities have been formed by two loves: the earthly by the love of self, even to the contempt of God; the heavenly by the love of God, even to the contempt of self"—the Cities of Jerusalem and Babylon (*City of God* XVI, 28; *Enarr.* in Ps. 64, 2).

The Christian view of history can be termed optimistic, but it is a tragic optimism that asserts itself in faith and holds onto hope in spite of the hard and painful reality of evil that is registered in our everyday experience as well as in our knowledge of the past. It is not pessimism but a healthy realism which grows out of something that is all too real, the presence of evil as a constitutive element in history.

This realistic view of things means that Christian thought can adopt the deep gravity of the Hellenic and Jewish pessimism, this sober view of man's destitution and tragedy which is a necessary ingredient of true wisdom. It enables us to reject with scorn the sickly platitudes of superficial optimism, the type that conservatives quite correctly denounce in the complacent verbalism of the Left, that way of counting on a sunny, brotherly future by concealing the horrors, hypocrisy and lies of the present with theoretical hope, the optimism of Dr. Pangloss: "All is for the best in the best of possible worlds at the present stage of human evolution and this will lead us infallibly toward the ideal we dream of."

We have learned to our cost what extreme cruelty and tyranny, from Saint-Just to Stalin, could be caused by this optimistic certainty that our course is set on the track that will lead humanity unwaveringly to the fulfillment of its destiny. Just a few more condemnations, purges, deportations and massacres, just one more step in the bloody mire of our present condition, and then we shall reach the kingdom, or the equivalent, or substitute. But I find I am beating my neighbor's breast in repentance instead of my own. It is not necessary to take examples from people outside the Christian tradition: we Christians have, unfortunately, quite enough to atone for! So many times in the past the millenarist temptation has triumphed and led to barbarous decisions, in order, if it were possible, to force the hand of history: witness, from 1661 to 1685 the policy that led to the revocation of the Edict of Nantes (just a few more companies of Dragoons and the whole of France would once more be united in the same faith!), or again, the anti-Catharist inquisition (just a few more heretics burned at the stake and Western Christianity will be without flaw!), or again, the long series of legal actions taken against the Jews which began in Spain with the Third Council of Toledo in 589 and spread through all the Christian kingdoms (just a little intimidation, a few forced baptisms, expulsions or banishments and this indomitable minority will be absorbed!).

However fervent our hope may be, we have no right to let it blind us. History is no triumphant ode leading the sons of Adam unfalteringly toward a promised horizon. We would have a clearer picture of the reality of history if we chose a polyphonic image: two themes run concurrently throughout the melody, sometimes one is dominant, sometimes the other, they are perpetually intertwined and contrasting with each other. There is the exultant theme of the City of God growing up little by little toward the joy of fulfillment, toward the *alleluia* of the Dedication. But it can only progress by threading its way through a thousand conflicts and persecutions and countless difficulties. At every step of the way the theme of the City of God is opposed by the theme of the enemy-city, or rather, by the innumerable contradictory and superimposed themes that we group under the one generic notion of the earthly city; for, as we have seen, the enemy-city is not built around one unifying principle. Evil is many-faceted.

The experience of the historian strikes a note of gravity. History does have a sinister, somber visage. Sin does exist. In fact, to our eyes, it is even more visible than grace, the motive force of history, for it is the irruption of sin into the world that marks the beginning of this fabric of suffering and mourning, the march of bloody, painful events (*City of God,* XIII, 14). As in each of our lives, the collective life of humanity is threaded with failures, work left undone, death that arrives just a moment too soon, error and sin. Violence reigns in the City, the just are oppressed and hypocrisy triumphs. If we consider only what we see with our eyes and touch with our hands, evil appears so much more prominently than good in the net balance of history! But we must not only take into consideration this one aspect of our experience. We have to look at it in conjunction with the vision that our faith gives us which reaches out to the obscure certainty of another reality.

12. THE AMBIVALENCE OF HISTORY

We only have to carry this analysis a little further to show the radical ambivalence of the time that we call history, not time considered as an abstract framework or context, a more or less basic category of being or of thought, but time lived, occupied and filled by the work and the doings of man. This lived-time is of a far more complex, ambivalent and ambiguous nature than modern optimism cared to admit when it so confidently extrapolated the evolution of technical progress and saw it only as a "factor of progress," making a veritable idol of change. To escape from this intoxication it would be well to listen to the wisdom of antiquity for a moment. For the ancients, those philosophers of being, change is not the fruitful process generating a higher quality of being which we, following in the footsteps of Hegel and Bergson, believe it to be. For the ancients, everything that comes into being through change is necessarily, by the same token, condemned to decline and death.

Aristotle has given an abstract analysis of this inevitable sequence with the dispassionate detachment of a biologist dissecting a specimen, in the treatise *On Coming To Be and Passing Away*. But from the pre-Socratic to the neo-Platonic thinkers, not everyone has been able to maintain the same impassiveness in face of this inexorable law. We already know how much St. Augustine was indebted to the neo-Platonists. His philosophy is also a philosophy of being; it would not be enough to say, of existence. For Augustine being that is truly being can only be the Eternal being. Permanency and immutability are its specific and supreme attributes. In a philosophy like this, time could never be envisaged as the bearer of only positive values (*De vera Relig.*, 21 [41]), it always appears as something of a scandal. Time is something fluid, elusive, in which being is received only in the fleeting moment, in the immediacy of the present which seems to be crushed between the past that is lost forever and a present that has not yet been given to us. To be, really and fully to be, one would have to be liberated from time, or at least from duration as man's sinful nature experiences it at present. Everything that happens in time as we live it does not possess *being* in the full sense of the word: "All that is borne away as it were by each instant which takes wing; things fall away like the flow of a mountain stream; no, our days *are* not: they have gone almost before they have come" (*Enarr. in Ps.* 38:7).

St. Augustine often used the paradox that Seneca was so fond of (*Ep. ad Lucil.*, 24:20: "we die every day, yes, each day takes part of our life from us . . ."; 26:4: "we are gradually worn away, each day takes away some of our strength"). Sometimes he uses a good deal of rhetorical hyperbole in his sermons, summoning all the well-tried resources of the classical diatribe, but he only does this to make his lesson strike home more surely. Of the goods of this earth, for instance, one must truthfully admit that "they are and, at the same time they are not; there is nothing stable in them; they slip away; they pour themselves out. Look at your grandchildren; you caress them and they caress you; but are they going to stay like that? You would be the first to want them to grow up and come of age. But you must realize that when a man reaches one age he dies to the age that preceded it. Yes indeed, when one reaches adolescence it is childhood that dies, and similarly at youth and at maturity; and then one reaches death." And further on he says: "Do you think that your children were born to live with you on earth, or rather so that they could drive you off it and take your place? . . . It seems that children, once they are born, say to their parents: 'Out! you must be ready to give way to us; now it is our turn to play our part,' for the life of the human race is like a drama on the stage" (*Enarr. in Ps.* 127:15).

One might mention innumerable texts in this vein, but I think it is sufficient to quote a passage from the *City of God* (XIII, 10) which is deservedly well-known: "For no sooner do we begin to live in this dying body, than we begin to move ceaselessly towards death. For in the whole course of this life (if life we call it) its mutability tends towards death. Certainly there is no one who is not nearer it this year than last year, and tomorrow than today, and today than yesterday, and a short while hence than now, and now than a short while ago. For whatever time we live is deducted from our whole term of life, and that which remains is daily becoming less and less; so that our whole life is nothing but a race towards death, in which no one is allowed to stand still for a little space, or to go somewhat more slowly . . ." Truisms? Yes, if you like. But the fact that this bitter truth has been repeated over and over again by the ancient philosophers, pagan and Christian alike, does not make it any less meaningful. Time is that fragile stuff with which the fabric of our lives is woven: "Tell me, Yahweh, when my end will be, how many days are allowed me, show me how frail I am" is the plea of Psalm 39 or, in Psalm 90: "Teach us to count how few days we have and so gain wisdom of heart."

What use do we make of the fragile stuff of time that has been entrusted to us for a moment? We must try to answer this question by looking at our own, personal lives. Who would dare to recount his life as a success-story grown more perfect every day? And I am not speaking of those unfortunate people who believe they can build their own life as though it were a work of art and make a success of it. "For anyone who wants to save his life will lose it . . ." (Mt 16:25 and parallels). Our bitter experience of everyday life has taught us that this saying is true. A man's life can seem very beautiful and successful from the outside, but the one who has to live it will always feel some bitterness when he looks back over his past. For is not everyone's past strewn with faults, errors and failures? If we measure what we actually do against the golden rule of what we should have done, our successes seem so ridiculously insignificant! Man never accomplishes more than a minute percentage of what he dreamed of doing, of what it was his duty to do. I believe I have known enough men of action intimately to be in a position to measure the meager results of all their efforts: I have seen the miscarriage of so many undertakings, the betrayals of so many hopes, so many achievements that are only caricatures of the original blueprint.

And if we turn from the field of action to the far more complex and meaningful domain of the inner life and man's spiritual ascent, we only have to listen to what some of the saints have told us. Thomas de Celano tells how, at the end of his life, Francis of Assisi said to his companions: "We should really begin to do something for the Lord, for up to now we have not made any real progress since the day of our conversion!" (*Leg.*, Ia, 6, 103), and Francis said this after receiving the stigmata at Alverno! From a human point of view it is difficult to conceive any higher sanctity. And yet he did not say this out of excessive humility or simply as a figure of speech. It was the straightforward expression of an agonizing experience, the experience of the abyss that separates man from the absolute for which he knows he was created.

And we find the same discordant note if we turn from the domain of man's inner, personal life, from a view of spiritual history on the personal level to the view of spiritual history on a collective level. The story of the Church throughout the ages bears witness to the same thing: the history of the major religious orders is marked by a succession of disciplinary and moral "reforms" whose effects eventually fade away and which then have to be undertaken all over again. A great many religious could sorrowfully say: "Our fervor has diminished considerably since the days of our holy founder." Even the Desert Fathers, in the middle of the fourth century, talked with longing of the days of St. Anthony and the first anchorites, those heroes of the ascetic life who had blazed the trail only one or two generations earlier and who now seemed impossible to imitate. And this is equally true of the Church as a whole: as Plato said of the ancients before him that they were greater because they had been nearer to the gods, so the Fathers of the Church are greater than we because they were nearer to Pentecost. It has been said[12] that, in a way, the Church will never again in the course of time (that is in the time of history as distinct form the eschaton) be so fervent, so full of love, so pure. That she will never again be as holy as on the blessed day of Pentecost when the Church consisted of the Virgin

[12] Charles Journet, *Destinées d'Israël*, Paris, Egloff, 1945, p. 112.

Mary and the little flock of Apostles. At that moment the Church was still unscathed by the first scandal which came so soon: the fraud attempted by Ananias and Sapphira appears in the fifth chapter of Acts.

The life of the Church, like that of the great religious orders, is marked by a succession of anxious examinations of conscience and attempts at reform which constantly have to be renewed and which are constantly in danger of being rendered powerless and ineffectual. We can see this very thing happening today with the *aggiornamento* so imperatively called for by the prophetic voice of John XXIII and so painstakingly set in motion during the deliberations of the Second Vatican Council. Today its fate is hanging in the balance between the impatience of some and the passive resistance of others, who rely on the mass of structures, traditions and reflexes inherited from the past.

Failure, at least a relative failure, is the law of all history, the theater of so many defeats in which even victories won at great cost are always precarious and partial. We must be capable of facing this truth. If our Christian faith is to avoid becoming completely insipid, it needs to be tempered by the experience of facing up to this sinister picture, of feeling the fearful wing of despair brush by. Only then can our faith profess, without embarrassment or illusions, that the divine plan of salvation is being accomplished through all the tragedies and suffering and apparent failures and is moving steadily toward fulfillment and triumph.

Such is the ambivalence of history! To the philosopher or theologian who attempts to explain it, it looks like a two-faced Janus of Roman mythology. One face is turned, with a smile, toward good and the fulfillment of being; the other, with a sinister grimace, toward evil, dissoluteness, destruction, non-being.[13]

[13] See H. I. Marrou, *l'Ambivalence du temps et de l'histoire, chez St. Augustin,* (Conférence Albert le Grand, Montréal, 1950), Institut d'Etudes Mediévales, Montréal, J. Vrin, Paris, 1950. R. Lorenz rendered the title, in German, as: *Das Janusantlitz der historischen Zeit,* in C. Andresen, *Zum Augustin-Gespräch der Gegenwart,* Darmstadt, 1962 (*Wege der Forschung,* V).

History is the matrix of the growing City of God. At the same time it is witness to the rotting away of the city of evil. But this city of evil is not so much an inert factor within the context of history as a static element of the human condition after the Fall. Sin also has dynamic energy of its own which works to expand the frontiers of its destructive action. This is so obvious to anyone who is willing to face reality that it is not even necessary to look for confirmation of it in revelation. We need only refer to the visceral wisdom of ancient humanity expressed in the myths that occur most frequently in ancient literature: Hesiod and the decline of the ages, the golden age that is lost for ever, the silver ages, the ages of bronze and iron and the harsh age in which we now live. If we read the Old Testament attentively we see a similar pattern: the fall, Cain, Lamech's violence, the corruption that led to the flood . . . and then the tower of Babel, and the whole cycle begins again. There is a decline or degeneration which seems to be the gradual explicitation of sin, as though there were a dark and sinister fecundity in evil.

Even such a brief perusal of the "illusion of progress" in which our forebears delighted will be sufficient to convince the reader of the radically ambivalent nature of the apparent victories of men. I shall not push the argument to the point of trying to establish a symmetry between progress and its concomitant signs of negation, as though the latter constituted a kind of counter-progress with meanings and values the exact opposite of those of the City of God, as though, with the growth of the City of God the earthly city necessarily plunged deeper and deeper into the slough of error and sin. As we have already seen, a careful reading of the *City of God* shows that a theology of history shuns such symmetry as a form of dualism. In the last analysis we do not know very much about it, and we should not be in too much of a hurry to transpose onto the level of dogma the images used in apocalyptic literature, which delights in depicting the forces of evil unleashed and apparently triumphant as the end of history draws closer: "And, after that, the whole world had marvelled and followed the beast . . ." (Rv 13:3f) This phrase elicited from St. Augustine the remark: "And what are we in comparison with those believers and saints who shall then exist?," who will be capable of resisting the onslaughts of the forces of evil unleashed upon them (*City of God*, XX, 8).

But we must not forget the Gospel account of the eschatological discourse just before the Passion: "False Christs and false prophets will arise and produce signs and portents to deceive the elect, if that were possible" (Mk 13:22; Mt 24:24) or earlier: "and with the increase of lawlessness love in most men will grow cold" (Mt 24:12). Also we must not forget the most impressive of these verses: "but when the Son of Man comes, will he find any faith on earth?" (Lk 18:8). We have to be careful to situate this logion in the correct context so as to avoid reading into it more than it really says or means in relation to the sum total of revelation. . . . But still, we cannot eliminate it, and the fact that it is there should be enough to make us suspect that the triumph promised to good will perhaps never be perceptible to empirical observation because of the effective presence of evil whose weight and strength will always be so strong. It is quite possible that on the eve of the supreme moment when history, having run its course, is about to come to an end, the mystical Body of Christ having reached the perfection of its full stature, it is quite possible that even at that moment the historian of institutions and technical developments and the witnesses of those days will see the earth as a field strewn with ruins and those days as a time of defeat.

13. THE MYSTERY OF HISTORY

The fact that history is ambivalent, combined with the fact that the real progress of the City of God is hidden and invisible to our eyes, leads to something of primary importance which we must now take the time to think about. It can be summed up in four words:

the mystery of history. It is significant that this expression seemed
to come absolutely naturally to theologians of such diverse inspiration
as Jacques de Senarclens[14] and Jean Daniélou[15], the former a
Calvinist from Geneva and the latter a French Jesuit! History is a
mystery—a *sacramentum,* to use the most ancient Christian, Latin
expression. It is a mystery in the sense that it is an object of revelation; that is, our knowledge of it is a participation in divine knowledge, although "by faith and not by sight" (2 Co 5:7). "Now we are
seeing a dim reflection in a mirror" (in the ancient mirrors of
polished bronze or silver the reflected image appeared as though in
a cloudy pool of water), "but then we shall be seeing face to face."
And St. Paul adds: "The knowledge that I have now is imperfect;
but then I shall know as fully as I am known" (I Co 13:12). He
insists very much on the partial, imperfect character of the knowledge of faith; the words "in part" are used three times in the verses
immediately preceding this one: "In part we know, in part we
prophesy," and "But once perfection comes all imperfect [partial]
things will disappear . . ." (I Co 13:9–10).

Revelation and faith certainly establish a communication between
man and God, between human knowledge and divine knowledge.
But God has revealed to us only as much as is necessary for our
salvation. Or, better, I should say that he has revealed to us all that
we are capable of knowing, given the nature of the human mind
and the nature of the object of revelation. This is the underlying
meaning of that obscure verse in Mark (13:32; see also Mt 24:36)
which has given rise to so much discussion amongst theologians:
"But as for that day or hour [of the end of time and history], nobody
knows it, neither the angels of heaven, nor the Son; no one but the
Father." It is not a question of a limitation of Christ's human knowledge but of an ontological impossibility for men still immersed
in history, to receive a full and complete communication of all
knowledge.

14 Jacques de Senarclens, *Le Mystère de l'histoire,* Geneva, 1949.
15 Jean Daniélou, *The Lord of History: Reflections on the Inner Meaning of History,* Chicago, Regenery, 1958.

Even if we are sure of being able to understand the overall meaning of history, this by no means implies that we are able to know and understand everything that happens in history as it happens. We can know "what history is *about*,"[16] we know the true object of history, but we are not able, in the here and now of our present situation, to decipher all the details of the ways and means that history takes to move towards its end. All we know is that this end will come. We do not know when and how. But we can understand why this knowledge is inaccessible to us: the innermost reality of history—the City of God, the mystical Body of Christ that is growing and being built up in time—is something which, by its very nature, is not accessible to the order of sensory experience and which therefore eludes us.

14. A CLERICAL HISTORY

Perhaps all this seems self-evident once we really think about it, but it was necessary to state it explicitly because even this elementary principle of an authentic Christian doctrine of history, has so often been completely obscured in the minds of the faithful or grossly distorted in the writings of inept apologists. Although it might be very enlightening this is not the time and place to launch into a list of all the distortions which this prudent and sound doctrine, first formulated by St. Augustine in his *City of God*, has been subjected to in the course of the centuries. Some of the most flagrant distortions have been formulated by well-meaning disciples, beginning with the faithful Orosis—typical of the enthusiastic but not very intelligent disciple—and continuing through the mediaeval chroniclers who were so skilful at interpreting the signs of the

[16] J. V. Langmead Casserley, *Toward a Theology of History*, Holt, Rinehart & Winston, New York, 1965.

heavens, down to Bossuet and even more recent apologists. To take only one example: a few years ago someone, animated by a zeal that was more pious than enlightened, thought he would honor the memory of the late Dom Guéranger by publishing four of his articles under the title *The Christian Meaning of History.* These articles had first appeared in 1858 in Veuillot's *l'Univers,* and in all fairness we have to judge them in their context. They were written as part of a polemical discussion, which is now quite obscure, directed against Prince Albert de Broglie's *History of the Church in the Fourth Century* which, in spite of its obvious goodwill toward Christianity, seemed to the good Benedictine to be infected with "naturalism." Of course we can share the indignation of the holy monk when he stresses the importance of the supernatural aspect of history and declares "that everything on this earth is for the chosen ones of God and the chosen are for Christ" (see 1 Co 3:22–23; one of Teilhard de Chardin's pet themes: all Christians are in communion with the same truth). We can also agree with him when, as heir to the great patristic heritage we have already mentioned, he says that, after Jesus Christ, a period of time still has to pass "of which no man possesses the secret because no man can know when the last of the chosen will be born." But we can no longer agree with him when he goes on to say: "Given this basic principle which has a divine certainty, history has no secrets for the Christian". . . "for he knows in advance that he cannot be mistaken"; "a Christian judges all facts, men and institutions from the point of view of the Church."

This was to confuse an authentic Christian view of the whole of History (capitalized!) with one known segment of the history of the Church. He identified God's point of view with that of the human beings who constitute the visible part of the Church and who, however well-meaning they may be, are still only men. Dom Guéranger chooses, amongst others, the example of Joan of Arc. He writes: "Faith shows us that this unprecedented manifestation of divine predilection for France points to the intention of saving the Most Christian Kingdom from the yoke of heresy that England would certainly have laid on her a century later." To this an English Catholic might humorously retort that God certainly does not love the British any less than the French and that if the Treaty of Troyes had been applied, the united kingdom of the Leopard and the Lily extending from the Tweed to the Mediterranean would have offered far greater resistance to the Reformation (supposing, of course, that the move toward Anglicanism was an unadulterated evil—which, for many good reasons, we are now seriously beginning to doubt!).

All this is only a caricature. God is, in the last analysis, the Lord of History, and he is leading everything according to his own good pleasure, toward its own end; that is absolutely certain. But he has not revealed the secrets of the ways he is following. We would have to be *in* God—the idea, in itself is inconceivable—in the very seat of his foreknowledge and providence, at the point where they become one in the "now" of his eternity, in order to decipher the mystery of history. So many saints remain totally unknown to us! So many deeds have had happy or tragic consequences that we are incapable of measuring or even foreseeing! Such and such an event, such and such an action, can seem to be catastrophic or beneficial for the Church at the time it occurs, whereas in reality, as later experience sometimes shows, the effects can be the exact opposite of what we thought. St. Augustine, for instance, finally resigned himself to the idea that the power of the Emperor should be vigorously exerted to bring the obstinate Donatist schismatics back to the fold. For a hundred years, from 312 to 411, every attempt had been made by the spoken and written word, in prose and in verse, to convince them of their error in disputing the validity of the election and consecration of Cecilian, Bishop of Carthage. Nothing had convinced them. But when severe measures were taken against them by the police or in the way of taxation, crowds of them came hurrying back to the arms of the Catholic Church they had been cursing so angrily . . .

How could anyone not be more than satisfied with such results? It is quite understandable. But the principle that was applied in this instance—that political power can effectively bring pressure to bear on men's religious conscience—was used three hundred years later to lead this same nation of North Africa to apostasy when temporal power passed into the hands of a Muslim master.

Or again—to take an example that is closer to our own times and that worked the other way—we could speak of the Roman problem that troubled Catholic consciences from 1860 until the Lateran Treaty: the fall of the Pontifical states and the annexation of Rome to the Italian Kingdom was seen, at the time, as a catastrophe and even a sacrilege. And yet, can we imagine what it would be like if Paul VI, in addition to having the charge of the Universal Church, had to administer Bologna and its communist electorate today?

15. HOLBEIN'S SKULL

Respect for divine transcendence is not the only reason why we should be on guard against this illusion which, although it is most assuredly a product of naïveté, is also a profanation—that of the so-called Christian historian who seems to be very much at ease in taking the place of God! A close analysis of the very structure of historical knowledge reveals how incomplete and partial, how very limited, our reconstruction of the past has been. It is not only faith it is also the science of the historian that is partial and imperfect. History, taken in its totality and its deepest reality, is also a mystery in the sense that we can never hope to acquire more than an extremely limited knowledge of it, owing to technical and gnoseological as well as ontological reasons. I have already expressed my thoughts on this subject at some length,[17] and so I shall make do with a brief summary here: technically an historian can never lay his

[17] H. I. Marrou, *De la connaissance historique,* Paris, Seuil, (Collection Esprit), 5th Edition, 1966.

hands on a documentation that is sufficiently complete, accurate and trustworthy to provide an answer to all the questions he has in mind. However limited the scope of any study, the documentation may be so abundant and difficult to decipher that one can never be certain of having exhausted all that it has to reveal, and in any event one can be even less certain of being capable of understanding it.

From the point of view of the theory of knowledge, history appears as an inextricable mixture of subject and object. The truth that is actually accessible to us is restricted by the particular, and therefore distorted, view which results from the historian's own personality and mental structures, his cultural background, and his curiosity, which determine the form of his questions and the elaboration of the answers he finds.

But even greater are the difficulties which arise from the very structure of historical being. Although our knowledge and experience of it is restricted, like the slim beam of a searchlight sweeping the dark night, it still affords us a glimpse of the extreme complexity of the structure of historical reality. There was a time when the historians' history seemed simple, for they dealt only with the political, diplomatic and military aspects of man's adventure. But the era of the history of the dates of battles is long past. For the last two centuries the development of a history of civilizations has led to an abundance of special histories: the history of Art—or rather history of the arts, for it is not easy to include the history of the plastic arts in the same embrace as, for instance, the history of music, which has its own determinism on the technical level and which, on the spiritual level, often seems to be behind the spirit of the times— the history of science, of ideas and mentalities, social and economic history. The popularity of the latter today can be largely explained by the fact that abundant documentation exists, especially for the recent past. We should beware of interpreting this as a sign of the naturally privileged position of economic history, as though once the economic aspects can be established in their rightful place, all the other contemporary aspects of human life will become intelligible for good measure.

It is true that a professional historian is often in a position to observe certain causal relationships or interactions between the different sectors of reality. But every true historian who has experienced the inexhaustible wealth and variety that can be discovered in the elements of any one period or milieu accessible to him, has also had occasion to learn that there is no fallacy more dangerous than the hypothesis which posits a unity between all the different contemporary manifestations of life comparable to that which governs a living body. This testimony of the practitioner is the solemn warning which the historian addresses to his brother the philosopher: now, more than ever before, it should be issued with urgency, for the temptation to bow down before this idol is reborn with every generation, like a phoenix rising from the ashes. Today can we not see Structuralism, which is so fashionable, gaily stepping into Spengler's shoes?[18]

Let us do a little quiet reasoning: if we generalize the notion of what is "technical"—as I have here, for the sake of convenience—and use it to designate all of the special aspects of human activity, one can see that the most diverse relationships are established in turn, between all the different technical aspects appearing at any one time in any given society: economic, political, religious, scientific, artistic, etc., and they can be relationships of coordination, subordination, independence or opposition, according to each case. In this way the object of history appears as an infinitely complex network of developments and causal series which are, turn and turn about, parallel, interwoven and intercommunicating. Each of these series or special aspects in turn can be seen to be complex in its structure, for different layers—sometimes ignoring each other, sometimes in alliance and sometimes in outright opposition—overlap and supersede each other like layers of silt from different periods of time and successive creative impulses.

---

[18] It is significant that the name of this teacher of somber error, the precursor of Nazism, should appear so spontaneously toward the end of Michel Foucault's *Les Mots et les Choses,* Paris, 1966, pp. 345 and 382.

We had already used the word "structure" earlier. Historical reality is not like loose powder: events, institutions, the phenomena of civilization are all interrelated and subordinate to each other in greater or lesser systems, although they can never be reduced to a total organic unity.

I remember I once had to initiate some students into the religious life of Roman North Africa of the third century. I had to show them how to recognize the superposition of at least five different layers, in the geological sense of the word. First the old Lybian foundation, our link with prehistoric times, then the Punic contribution, the Greek influences, the clearly visible and massively documented layer of the Roman period and finally, like a thin, frail film overlying the whole structure, the traces of the "new religiosity," pointing to the future—the advent of religions of Eastern origin, and first amongst them Christianity. What we studied there was a very brief period that could almost be taken in at one glance, and we were concerned only with the religious aspect of that Roman-African civilization. The ethnic, demographic, political, economic and artistic structures of this period would have demanded a much more attentive study, as much for themselves as for the purpose of determining how they stood in relationship to each other.

It is true that historical experience has its own particular fecundity. The professional historian can testify to the human, cultural enrichment he has gained in the practice of his art. But this experience—and I apply this equally to the historian of the past and to the man of action in the present, for their experiences go to confirm each other—this experience culminates in an admission of powerlessness insofar as the problem of the meaning of history is concerned.

Without revelation we could say absolutely nothing about this with any certainty. One after another, when our turn comes, we all climb onto the stage of history to play the brief part that has been assigned to us by the limitations of our lives. It is not easy for anyone to have an overall idea of the drama which is being acted out and in which his part lasts for only one brief moment and absorbs the whole of his being. We are like the extras with a walk-on part, waiting in the wings for our turn to go on. Puzzled and astonished, we watch the immense crowd of actors and dancers coming and going on the stage. Seen from the wings (unfortunately none of us are in the orchestra seats where, in imagination, the ingenuous philosopher of history is sitting comfortably, watching the play) the meaningful, overall pattern of these comings and goings escapes us. All we can see is a distorted foreshortening. If I may be permitted to use an image to illustrate this, it is a little like that mysterious skull that the genius of Holbein throws at the feet of his two *Ambassadors*: it is so distorted and twisted that it is all but unrecognizable.

16. HISTORY THAT IS INVISIBLE

So far we have considered only the most visible aspects of historical life, which we can most easily grasp: economic, political, artistic, the exterior forms of religious life. . . . However, we know by now that true history takes place on another level. History is the construction of the holy City, the growth of the Body of Christ. We have some idea of the dark depths of this mystery. Only at the eschaton, when we know as we are known, shall we be capable of sharing in the divine thought and seeing the ascending movement of that history which is more than real. The fact that we know that true history takes place on the spiritual level, on the level of the supernatural life, does not make us capable of grasping it and describing it. In this area almost more than in any other, ambivalence and ambiguity threaten our meager human knowledge. There are so many false triumphs and so many triumphant failures in what we can see of history! The contribution which each one of us, with the help of grace, makes to the maturing of time usually remains almost completely unknown and even, because of its transpsychological substance, doubly unknown. St. Augustine explained this one day in a sermon: like the Incarnate Word during his human life—except for the day of the Transfiguration—the members of his Body are both visible, in their appearance, and invisible, in their hidden value (*Serm. Mai, 14, 3*). What they are in reality, what they are worth, what they do, is kept a secret and, for the time being, is known only to the Father. Their life is hidden with Christ in God (Col 3:3). Their true work, the part they have played in the coming of the kingdom, usually remains completely inaccessible to us. It is only at the Day of Judgment that it will be seen in the light of day. Then the pagans will cease their calumnies and glorify God for the things that have been accomplished (I P 2:12). Only very exceptionally and when necessary for the good of the Church, does God allow the holiness of one of his sons to be seen and to give rise to a cult or canonization, which sets him up as a model for our imitation and a source of intercession. Normally the saints remain hidden. There is something very profound in the belief which was dear to both cabalistic Judaism and the mystical segments of Islam concerning the "just ones," the "saints" who are hidden, and "it is because of them that the world subsists." Of course these theories went too far in their claims to penetrate the secret purposes of God, but it seems that the error lies especially in the fact of determining the number of the saints: thirty-six in the Jewish tradition, three hundred and fifty-five, plus four thousand who are counted as saints even though they do not know it themselves, in Sufism.[19] But men cannot claim to know in advance how far divine mercy will reach or how rich will be the yield of grace. All of us can hope to be one of the just who were missing from Sodom. Basically, however, this thesis is correct: as the second-century Apologists liked to proclaim: "What the soul is in a body, this the saints (or, the terms are interchangeable: the Christians) are in the world. . . . As the soul holds the body together, so Christians hold the world together" (*Ep. to Diogn.* 6: 1,

[19] See the references I have mentioned in my edition of the *Epistle to Diognetus*, Paris, 2nd ed., 1965 (Sources chrétiennes, vol. 33 bis), p. 154.

7). This was the language of the Stoics: they speak of the Christians as containing, sustaining, maintaining the world, as a principle of interior cohesion, unity, permanency and life for the world.

No man, nor even the militant pilgrim Church, has received the power to read the details of history. By faith we are in communion with its overall movement, but we are not in a position to form a judgment on the exact function of each event, the degree of negative or positive participation of every actor on the scene or of any one of his deeds, in the ongoing process of history. We cannot always make out what has worked, and is at present working, to hasten the coming of the kingdom. God's ways are impenetrable. In a mysterious way he can even use evil to further his purposes.

When St. Augustine calls attention to what, in our theology, corresponds to the "wiles of reason" of Hegelian philosophy, the example that seems to occur to him spontaneously is the capture of Jerusalem and the destruction of the Temple by the Roman Legions in the year 70. Could Titus know that by this act he was fulfilling the Prophecy of the Little Apocalypse? Let us stick to what Scripture tells us explicitly in the case of King Cyrus: on a Babylonian cylinder seal is the boast: "[Marduk] sought out a just king; he held out his hand to the man of his heart; he called Cyrus, King of Anshan, by his name; he called his name to a universal reign . . ."[20]. But like all ambitious men who build an Empire and who shout out in victory: "God is on our side," Cyrus is deceiving himself. Listen to what the Prophet says; it is the Second-Isaiah who is speaking, and he is addressing the King Cyrus: "it is for the sake of my servant Jacob, of Israel my chosen one, that I have called you by your name, conferring a title though you do not know me. . . . Though you do not know me, I arm you that men may know from the rising to the setting of the sun that, apart from me, all is nothing" (Is 45:5–6). Or again, to take an example from the New Testament, we can see, in the eleventh chapter of the *Letter to the Romans*, what Paul says about Israel's refusal to recognize Jesus

[20] See E. Schrader, *Keilinschriftliche Bibliothek*, III, 2, p. 122.

Christ as the Messiah they were waiting for: he explains that Israel has stumbled and fallen, and yet this evil is mysteriously linked with the salvation of the Gentiles and the hope of salvation for the world: "How rich are the depths of God—how deep his wisdom and knowledge—and how impossible to penetrate his motives or understand his methods!" (Rm 11:33).

17. INTERTWINED

We come now to one of the most essential and profound aspects of our doctrine, which has been set forth with special clarity in the teaching of St. Augustine. It was not enough to learn to distinguish the two cities and the battle that rages between them. It was also necessary to have a clear idea of the relation in which they stand to each other insofar as we can, in fact, see this in the experience of history. Their relationship is complex because "these two cities are entangled together in this world (like the strands of wicker in a woven basket), and intermixed (like a chemical emulsion) until the last judgment effects their separation . . ."(*City of God*, 1, 35). This formula is understandably renowned, and St. Augustine himself often used it with good reason in other contexts (see *City of God* XI, 1; XIX, 26; *de Gen. ad litt.* XI, 15 [20]; *Enarr. in Ps* 61, 8; 64, 2; 136, 1; *de Catech. rud.*, 19 [31]). This idea of inextricable intertwining, commingling, is one of the fundamental principles of the Christian theology of history. It can be drawn quite naturally from the parable of the darnel and the wheat. (Mt 13:24–30. For the explanation of the parable see vv 36–43). St. Augustine himself came back to this parable again and again whether in his polemical discussions with the Donatists and, later, with the Pelagians or in his ordinary preaching for the good people of Hippo (*Enarr. in Ps* 149, 3; *in Ps* 64, 16–17; *Serm. Caillau St. Yves*, 11, 5).

In the householder's field—and this field is the world in which our history is taking place—the good grain (that is, the sons of the Kingdom) and the poisonous weed (that is, the sons of the Evil One) grow up side by side, so inextricably mixed that even the Lord's angels dare not weed out the darnel for fear of uprooting the growing wheat at the same time. We have to wait until the cosmic day of harvest comes round, when time and history will be accomplished, before they can finally be separated from each other.

One can easily see the practical consequences of a doctrine such as this. Anyone who has fully understood it could never have a "Manichean" image of the world in which the just, God's side, are lined up on one side and the wicked on the other; the just being assured of attaining the Kingdom, the others already condemned. The dividing line between the two cities is, in practice, invisible to our eyes. How many times Augustine comes back to this in his preaching! It is true, he found many occasions to do so in the Gospel. Apart from the parable of the darnel and the wheat there is the one of the fishing net cast out to sea, which brings into the Church both the just and the wicked (Mt 13:47–50; see the hundred and fifty-three fishes of the last miraculous catch: Jn 21:11). There is also, in John the Baptist's preaching, the image of the threshing floor on which the grain and the chaff are still mixed (Mt 3:12 and Lk 3:17). No! It is not easy for us, in our present context, to distinguish the elect from the damned. Amongst those who hate the Church there are some who are chosen and do not know it, whereas amongst those who go to church and frequent the sacraments there are some who will never share the eternal destiny of the saints (*City of God* I, 35, etc.). One could give an indefinite number of references in this connection.

Let us go back, for example, to that admirable *Sermon Caillau St. Yves,* 11, 5, in which St. Augustine calls on the faithful: "You are the grain, the ears, the wheat of Christ. Look into your conscience: if you find that you are wheat, pray for final perseverance; if you find that you are a mixture of wheat and darnel, look to change yourselves. . . . The enemy has sown darnel everywhere:

laymen, clergy, bishops, married people, religious men and women, he has left no area untainted."

To equate the history of the City of God which is always, in a large measure, invisible to our sight, with what we can see of the history of the visible Church would be a grotesque caricature of our theology. This misunderstanding, as we have already seen, has often occurred, however, from Orosis or Otto de Freising to Bossuet and Dom Guéranger. Claiming to write a history of the City of God, many have been content, in fact, to write an "ecclesiastical" history (to borrow the expression from Butterfield, the English historian). A Frenchman would more readily speak of a "clerical" history, but it would be more accurate (if I may be pardoned the mediaeval frame of reference) to speak of a "guelfic" history.

It is certainly not a question of denying the sanctity of our Mother the hierarchic Church, nor her fruitfulness and her mysterious capacity for producing saints. But her inner visage, her real beauty, can only be seen by her divine Lord. Her true vitality is not something that can be measured by sociological studies—even if the latter are invaluable on their own level to guide the faltering steps of pastoral activity.

Our doctrine of the ambivalence of history can be applied very fruitfully here. On the one hand it is true that the Church is the people of the "chosen saints"—or "those who are called to be saints"—and that the Spirit dwells in the Church, assists her and will always be victorious over the powers of darkness within her. On the other hand it is no less true, alas, that from an empirical point of view the Church appears as composed of sinners and sensual men, not to mention the ignorant whose good will turns out to be sterile for lack of technical skill and the bunglers who aim for the wrong goals and are skillful only at letting the historic occasion slip by . . .

The two cities are intertwined one in the other. An historian who is aware of his responsibility would never venture—unless he received a private revelation, and who could make such a claim!—to evaluate the contribution to the coming of the Kingdom made by any episode or major event in history, by any one act of any one man or even of the total destiny of that man, or by a whole era, people or civilization. Who could ever claim to measure accurately the percentage of those who can be counted as citizens of the City of God and the percentage of those who are citizens of the city of evil in any given instance?

Already, as time goes on and puts a distance between ourselves and certain events in history, we realize that even though men who were contemporary to a given event may have judged it at the time as being all good or all evil, we have to be far less categorical in our judgment of it. We have already mentioned a few typical instances: the repression of Donatism and the whittling away of the Papal States until all that was left was the symbolic Vatican City. An example closer at hand would be the separation of Church and State established by the French law of 1905. When this law was first promulgated our forebears saw it as a catastrophe and a persecution, a terrible threat hanging over the future of the Church of France (and in fact the most ardent advocates of the law intended it as such). In practice, it has revealed many positive aspects. Today we are far more sensitive to the autonomy and liberty that the Church obtained through this law and we have no special longing for the Church of the Concordat! Can we imagine what it would be like today if, during an economic depression, we had to fight for permission from the Ministry of Finance to create new parishes so desperately needed for the development of pastoral work?

Here again we come up against the notion of ambivalence in attempting to draw a clear line around the borders of the Church. Where does it begin and where does it end? How do people belong to this great body, to this unity? Can we ever really define it? We can put our finger on a good many achievements in history in which we can be fairly sure of recognizing a positive contribution to the building up of the City of God, whatever the percentage of darnel that can always be seen, mixed with the wheat. Such are the work of institutions which, in retrospect, can be seen to conform to the spirit of the Gospel—and which, in fact, have often borne fruit under the indirect influence of the Gospel—but which did not come about within the ordinary functions of the visible Church. In fact, to be quite frank, many of them came about in spite of persistent opposition from the majority of those who represented the official functions of the Church and who constituted what the sociologist would call the "Christian milieus." An excellent example of this, cited by H. Butterfield, is the whole question of religious freedom, which has only just been assimilated by the body of the Church and that with great difficulty. Another example is that of the improvements in the sphere of social justice won by the long struggle of the worker movements. After all, it must have been easy to preach on the great dignity of the poor in the Church, in front of the land-owning aristocracy of Antioch or the silk-clad courtiers of Versailles. I cannot see that it would have called for too much boldness if one's name was Chrysostom or Bossuet. How can the historian help seeing most of these appeals as a farce simply because they were completely ineffectual, technically speaking, in view of fallen human nature marked by sin and, especially, by the curse attached to Mammon? The worker movement only succeeded in wresting a few shreds of justice from the ruling classes because it managed to instill fear into them. Those who made up the ruling classes, even if they thought of themselves as Christian, were pagans in this respect. The violence of the workers broke down their defenses and forced them to practice the justice that the preaching of the Gospel had never managed to win from them. Would anyone venture to say, now, that this increase in justice and decrease in oppression (even if the results are still so limited) should not be counted as a positive contribution to the coming of the Kingdom?

Of course all these estimates are conjectural. But the very fact that they can be brought to the attention of the Christian conscience is enough to warn us against constructing a simple equation between what we are and what we should be, between the visible Church disfigured by the sin of its members and the invisible progress of the Church and, with it, the progress of the whole of humanity toward the fulfillment of history. The Gospel saying, "judge not" should be applied to two levels of experience: the level of the past and the level of our own inner life. The professional experience of the historian shows him the "polyphonic" structure of true history, of the whole of history, and its sequence built up, as it is, of complex casual relations. He can understand to what extent the judgment of men can be empty and relative. By attempting to judge history men usurp the privilege of the eschatological Judge, for no man alive can ever really appreciate the ultimate consequences of any event in history, the unforeseen results that it sets in motion and, ultimately the only thing that really matters, its effect in hastening or in delaying the coming of the Kingdom.

18. OUR HEART IS DIVIDED

Similarly we know from our most intimate personal experience that this ambivalence, this "perplexity"—if I may be allowed a play on the etymological sense of the word, in the manner of the rhetorical orators of antiquity—lies deep in each one of us. I wish . . . I would like to . . . I think I want to consecrate myself wholly to the service of the Lord and of the holy City. And yet, at the same time, I am constantly aware of my infidelity to this fundamental option. I never seem to be converted except on the surface of my being. Whether by cowardice or weakness or by complicity with evil I do not really accomplish the good that I would like to and that I know I am capable of accomplishing. Worse still, I often do the evil that I do not want to do (we pray for forgiveness for the sins that remain hidden even to our own eyes: "Wash out my hidden faults," Ps 19:12)—by unconscious connivance with the collective sins of my social class, of my race, of my times. As Cardinal Journet has often reminded us in his preaching,[21] the front line of the battle

---

[21] Ch. Journet, *l'Eglise du Verbe incarné,* Paris, 1951, vol II, p. 1 103, 1 315 As. v. *City of God;* vol I, (s.d., p. 224). *Nova et Vetera,* 33 (1958) p. 30; 38 (1963) p. 302.

between the Church and the world, between light and darkness, between the City of God and the city of evil, cuts through *our own* hearts.

This is admirably said, and it seems to me to be a legitimate commentary on the teaching of St. Augustine in his *City of God.* Also it adds a useful dimension to his teaching which was developed mainly from a collective and social point of view.

Augustine notes, for example, that the wicked fight amongst themselves—the spectacle of rival empires taking up arms against each other is common in history—and that the wicked and the just also fight each other. This is the normal course of history. Christ never promised his faithful that they would triumph tomorrow, or on any earthly tomorrow. He promised them persecution and martyrdom. Finally Augustine begins to wonder whether the just, too, can war amongst themselves, and he comes to the conclusion that they would not do so, in fact they would be incapable of doing so, if they were entirely perfect. However, at best, they are only on the way to perfection, and this is why they do wage war amongst themselves. With a perfectly clear conscience every man attacks the very real evil he sees in the other, in the name of the good he himself is pursuing (*City of God* XV, 5).

This explains why conflicts amongst Christians are so fierce: as a Frenchman I have had painful daily experience of the conflict between Catholics of the Right and those of the Left. It is true, we are, quite literally, incapable of understanding each other because the evil we all see in our adversaries is all too real. These relentless struggles are an intolerable scandal. How can we dare to open the *Gospel of St. John* at his statement of the ultimate criterion for our common belonging to Christ: "By this love you have for one another, everyone will know that you are my disciples" (Jn 13:35). We must try to do away with the scandal of division in every possible way and with all the energy we can muster. And yet, on the other hand, we must also recognize that it is written into the very law of history. In a sense, we shall never be rid of it until the last day, the last victory.

The unity that Christ's teaching enjoins so unequivocally can never be fully realized until the coming of the eschaton when, finally cured of the ills that afflict us, we shall attain perfection. Until such time it can only be partial and a caricature of itself. The experience of history is there to vouch for this. Only in very exceptional circumstances and in view of a limited and clearly defined goal have all the faithful, the conscious members of the visible Church, been able to gather together in one undertaking, with a view to attaining one objective. And even when this has been possible the coalitions thus formed have rapidly found themselves weighed down by serious doubts and basic ambiguities. We can see this clearly in the innumerable attempts to form Christian political parties. . . . One example is sufficient to illustrate this: to meet the challenge of the *Kulturkampf* and resist Bismarck's hostile policies German Catholics felt the necessity of banding together to form a political party in opposition. At first this seemed to be very effective, but later parliamentary power play led to many compromises during the period of the Weimar Republic until its overthrow by Hitler.

This mystery of history adds a certain note of tragedy to our existence. Our actions are being carried out in a twilight zone which is only dimly lit by very broad principles drawn from faith and the Church's teachings. We are often torn between two sets of categorical imperatives in contradiction with each other. We are bound to inform our consciences, and yet we have to make our own decisions and respond, each for himself, to the demands of our own vocation in life. I would like to take an example which has the advantage of being far enough away for us to be able to look at it dispassionately: the Roman question. We can imagine the difficult position of Italian Catholics after 1860–1870, torn between their loyalty to the Pope and their right, or rather their duty, to their country.

It is important to realize that this was not just an unfortunate accident due to a particularly ill-assorted constellation of circumstances or, as the saying went in those days, "the evils of the age."

Can any period of history be said to have avoided the curse of being called "evil" (Ep 5:16)? No, I must insist on this: the conflict is characteristic of our historical condition. History is not bestowed upon us like an object that we can get to know and contemplate from without. We have no heavenly belvedere from which we can look down on history and sum it all up in a few well-chosen words. What a diabolical temptation for a Christian to picture himself transported to the mountain top, from which he could survey all the kingdoms of the earth laid out at his feet! We are not onlookers, we are woven into the fabric of history, swept along by the current, active and passive, enduring but also creating it. It is impossible for us to know history, for it has not yet been written.

19. MUSICAL TIME

I would now like to refer to what I have proposed to term the musical conception of historical time, a theory which St. Augustine has expounded in two very important works. These are two letters: one addressed to Marcellinus, for whom he wrote the *City of God* as a reply to the objections raised by the educated pagans of Carthage (Ep 138, 1 [5]); the other to St. Jerome, in which he discusses the heartrending question raised by the death of a baby (Ep 166, 5 [13]). St. Augustine liked to imagine the course of history as an exquisite song (see *City of God* XI, 18). This was not simply a way of expressing his optimistic judgment on the world and its future with the use of an aesthetic image: it is a close comparison. We can see this if we compare it with the analysis which Augustine, following the musicological tradition of Aristoxenus of Tarentum, made of musical time and our perception of it. A melody begins, a fugue takes it up, a symphony unfolds its treasures one by one. All the elements, notes, movements and harmonies of a piece of music follow on each other in a temporal sequence. As they are played they are perceived by the listener and etch themselves on his memory until, little by little, he begins to build up a perception of the whole, a musical judgment constituting the sense and significance of the work. But he cannot have this judgment or sense of a piece of music when it begins—unless, of course, the piece has no musical substance and is just a bugle call that follows a clearly foreseeable pattern. The meaning of a piece of music, its very being, is finally established only when the last movement of the fugue has been played, the last chord struck; when the last cadenza has died away. Until then the melody can always rise again, be modulated, develop in a new direction, take on a new vitality and be enriched with new harmonies—witness the ambiguous modes of the Gregorian melodies which declare themselves only in their conclusion.

We can imagine that history unfolds according to a somewhat similar pattern. God, the creator of the universe, is also the one who orders and rules the unfolding of time, and history can with some truth be compared to an immense concert conducted by the all-powerful hand of God. Only he knows where it is going. It is not yet established. Like the piece of music it can always rise again and be renewed. It will only possess its full meaning once it has come to an end. In the final analysis this is the ultimate explanation for the existence of what I have called the mystery of history. It has not yet been accomplished. It is in the process of becoming itself and we are contributing to this. We can vouch for the fact that it does have meaning and, thanks to revelation, we can even see the overall content of its progress—filling up the ranks of the City of the saints, the growth of the Body of Christ—but we cannot describe it as an object, something that can be placed before us. What an insipid notion of God must have prevailed in the minds of the philosophers of history who thought, in their presumption, that they could contemplate the whole panorama of universal history and explain it all!

At this point it is a simple matter to show that, in the last analysis, the mystery of history implies the mystery of our freedom. In fact it is really the same mystery. For the time being and as long as we continue to live in faith we must remain in ignorance of the details of how history is reaching fulfillment. But this is not because God has chosen, let us say for pedagogical reasons, to test us, to hide something that he could have revealed to us. It is because history is also subject to the free exercise of man's liberty, and it is indeterminate for the time being simply because it is formed by the free decisions which men are taking today and still have to take in the future. Nothing is established yet. Consequences that we can foresee as being highly probable in any one area may not come about. At each turn in the path of time new undertakings can cause the exquisite melody, which seems to be drawing to a close in a foreseeable pattern, to spring to life again and develop new harmonies.

Here again, the experience of an historian can illustrate this general proposition with some concrete examples: he knows that history is unpredictable by its very essence; dramatic and unexpected turns of events, paradoxical consequences, are the rule. At any moment, the most firmly established chain of cause and effect can be disrupted by the unexpected appearance of new factors. The true historian—one who has virtually become a contemporary of the period he has studied, reliving their events—will inevitably protest against the simplistic belief of the philosopher that the reasons for certain events are, in retrospect, so perfectly clear and obvious that what happened could not have been otherwise. This is simply not so. The smallest grain of sand could have clogged up the mechanism of cause and effect—Cleopatra's nose, had it been shorter!—and things would have developed differently. And in the same way today history is still going on. It will only give up its secret when its time has run out, when all the causes have exhausted their possibilities of effect, when all men's decisions have been made and have borne their fruit. But this is, in a way, a negative point of view, and it is not the only one from which we can observe the mysterious unfolding of history.

20. IN CONTACT WITH GOD

I do not know whether the name of Leopold von Ranke (1795–1886) will mean very much to most of my readers, so I shall do them the favor of reminding them that he was not only one of the great minds of German letters but also, in my opinion, the first great modern historian in the scientific sense of the word. He was the first to realize that one must work on primary sources (he began with the archives of the Republic of Venice); at the same time, he showed himself to be the great artist that the writer of history must be if the truth, in all its subtle varieties and shades, that he has unearthed as a scholar is to be communicated to the world without being distorted or betrayed. In a lecture given in 1854[22] he coined the well-known maxim: every period is directly in touch with God, every generation is equidistant from eternity.

For von Ranke, this formula expresses the protest of the professional historian which I discussed earlier. He clung to the specific values of his discipline and attacked Hegel and the philosophy of history in general because of the abuse of the notion of progress to which it leads. If one is, above all, aware of the whole trajectory of humanity he will have a tendency to see each civilization and each period as simply one more step toward the final outcome. If each generation is seen only in its mediacy it no longer has its own particular significance. It is simply one rung in the ladder of progress. But the historian knows from experience that his study of any one period is fruitful and fascinating and that it possesses its own values which are sometimes of inestimable worth. I cannot imagine anyone saying, for instance, that the "Primitives" were nothing more than a period of transition between the Middle Ages and the Renaissance!

[22] Leopold von Ranke, *Ueber die Epochen der neueren Geschichte,* (Weltgeschichte IX, 2).

Marx was sufficiently cultured to have experienced a difficulty in this respect. His problem was that Homer, and the art of Greece as a whole, seemed to him to possess permanent aesthetic value independently of the forms of social development in which they arose. They had, as it were, an absolute value.

But von Ranke's formula, which has often been repeated and sometimes misinterpreted, can also be understood in a more profound sense. In the general perspective of our theology of history it can be used to express the mysterious relationship between time and eternity, or, better, between history and eschatology.

The apocalyptic style, in which the prophet's judgment of the present or of the immediate future and his foresight of the last days are condensed into one all-embracing vision, has often been discussed. The time of history is all but eliminated by a foreshortening of perspective, the vast stretches of the centuries disappears and the eschaton appears on the near horizon. Take the example of the oldest of the canonical Apocalyptic books, the *Book of Daniel*. To read it, it would seem that the eschatological Kingdom (2:44), the coming of the Son of man (7:13) and the Last Judgment (12:1f) will all follow immediately on the death of the persecutor, Antiochus Epiphanes. This pattern repeats itself in the "Little Apocalypse" of the Synoptic Gospels, but this time it is the sack of Jerusalem by Titus that is inextricably mixed up with the picture of the end of time. The same can be said of the *Book of Revelation*. I would like to disregard, for a moment, the characteristic significance of all prophecy: Antiochus Epiphanes and First Century Rome are types which can be found in any pagan State that persecutes men, at whatever moment in history it may appear. I shall disregard, also, the fact that this type of literature is an expression of God's goodness: by such means he calls our attention to the coming of the last hour in order to exhort us to watch and pray.

These writings cannot be explained simply as a pedagogical stratagem or a literary form. The systematic link which they establish between the present as it is lived by the prophet's contemporaries and the end of time puts a very profound truth before us—"insinuates" as the Fathers liked to say, a very profound truth—for our reflection. It is true that each successive episode in history fits into place, the place known and willed by God, in the fabric of the history of mankind. Each incident has its appointed place in this long journey —now I may use the word: this long pilgrimage—that starts with Creation and the Fall and leads to the Last Judgment. Every historical adventure marks a new phase of the destiny, the becoming of man, like recurring notes stressing the rhythmic unfolding of the great symphony which we cannot perceive with our senses but which, by faith, we know to exist in reality and to develop in mysterious harmony.

And this is true of the brief episode of each of our lives which seems so small a fragment when looked at in the framework of universal history. This brief terrestrial journey lived, by turns, in exertion, suffering, temptation, a little joy and hope, takes us to the hour which will be our last from an earthly point of view. Death is the beginning of the End for each one of us. It is always close at hand threatening us while a "thousand fall at your side, ten thousand at your right hand," so that the present is always, as it were, surrounded by the tragic light of the universal End and, by the same token, is charged with eschatological values.

It is in this very profound sense that we can echo von Ranke's dictum that every period and every generation in history, and each one of our personal lives, is directly in touch with God and eternity, with the "beyond" in which history reaches its fulfillment. For what is true of our own personal lives is true of the whole of history, the collective adventure of the human race. This reminds me of the inscriptions on some old sun-dials: *vulnerant omnes, ultima necat*: every hour that we live brings us closer to our last hour. In a way we can say that as each hour advances the words of the apostles become a little more literally true, a little more directly applicable: "The night is almost over, it will be daylight soon" (Rm 13:12); "Brothers, this is what I mean: our time is growing short" (I Co 7:29); "Only a little while now, a very little while" (He 10:37); "Everything will soon come to an end" (I P 4:7): "Children, these are the last days" (I Jn 2:18); "I shall indeed be with you soon" (Rv 22:20).

It would be more accurate to say that these words have always been true: one cannot help being struck by the frequency with which the affirmation recurs throughout the New Testament. It would be ingenuous to try and "explain" it away as the expression of the obsessive conviction the first generation of Christians had of the proximity of the Parousia. However, hypothetical such a psychological reconstruction of the times may be, the important, dominating fact is that these texts were accepted by the Church as part of the inspired canon of Scripture. They must, therefore, be true, with a truth that is, as it were, permanent, and as valid for every generation of Christians as for the first generation.

For every civilization and every generation of men, just as for every man alive, it must be admitted that the Last Day of the world is his last day; one could even say his only day, for what is the length of a man's life or even the length of a period of civilization, compared not only to eternity but even to the immense length of the whole of human history? This is the metaphysical perspective underlying the constitution *Benedictus Deus* by which Benedict XII corrected John XXII's imprudent statements concerning the fate of the souls of the just before the Last Judgment. The Good Thief began his reign with the Son of Man on the very evening of Good Friday. "Today you will be with me in paradise." As St. Ambrose expresses it so well: "Life is to be with Christ, for where Christ is, is Life and the Kingdom" (*In Lucam* X, 121).

Eschatology is always there, for each one of us, on the horizon of our own life. After all, what did it matter to the martyrs in the days of the Maccabees that Nero and Diocletian were to come after Antiochus IV . . . and after them, Stalin and Hitler? The path of the martyrs and of every man, the path that I take, appears to be a real but infinitesimal segment of the curve described by the whole of history. Year by year—the years that are given to me to work in the vineyard of the Lord, the years that I squander in sin, the years in which, too, the work of grace grows deeper and stronger within me—the words of the Apostle, "our salvation is even nearer than it was when we were converted" (Rm 13:11) become more literally true for me. The passing of time brings me imperceptibly closer to that last hour which is as unforeseeable as the "End of the World," when, my practical participation in the work of history being accomplished, I shall break out of the bounds of time to fall at the feet of the sovereign Judge. It is hardly surprising that something of the gravity of this hour can already be seen in each present moment of our lives.

But this truth can also be invested with a more profound meaning. The Last Day, the "eschaton," is not just an instant in the time sequence, a given day in a given year that has its date assigned according to the chronological measurement in use with the historians of the moment. The Last Day is also the total accomplishment of God's purpose for his creation. And yet, although it is true that this final accomplishment will only be achieved on that great Day, it would be a mistake to imagine that it is exclusively reserved for that day. In reality the accomplishment of God's purpose accompanies and sustains the duration of history. It is always present in history, gathering the fruit of every tear and of every outpouring of love. In this way it can be said that the whole of time shares and is clothed in the dignity of the eschaton.

For nor can Christian history be reduced simply to a succession of instants measured by clocks and chronicles. As Augustine saw very clearly (*City of God* XI–XII, 9. These chapters treat of the "prologue in heaven" in which the duration of human history recognizes its kinship with the mysterious becoming of angelic history), in a much fuller sense, time is the mode of accomplishment of the divine purpose which will be brought to fulfillment at the eschaton. It is the accomplishment in depth (in the density of being), and it is a reality that is mysterious, like everything that has to do with being, but of which we can gain a glimpse with the help of the inspired metaphors of "growth," "maturation" and "building the edifice."

21. THE CHURCH OF HEAVEN

Before we develop these fundamental truths any further I would like to emphasize one aspect which we cannot neglect with impunity and which so many of our contemporaries, even many Christians, spontaneously run the risk of neglecting. I mentioned in passing that the visible participation of each one of us in the total picture of history—construction of the City of God, growth of the Body of Christ—comes to an end whether he be martyr, saint or sinner, with his last hour and the end of his brief sojourn on this earth. We should underline the word *visible,* for we cannot forget the absolutely essential part played by the prayers of the saints, who are so clearly shown in the Book of Revelation in the place reserved to them.

Men who are still on earth are not alone in their combat for God. St. Augustine always stressed the fact that the Church of Heaven, the angels and the saints, stand alongside and above what we usually call the militant Church. In the Creed we confess belief not only in our expectation of the Resurrection but also in the communion of the saints. The saints have not been put on the shelf until the end of history. They are not content simply to wait, relegated to some mysterious reservoir as the apocalyptic literature of later Judaism liked to imagine—even describing its fantastic geography (I Enoch 22:8–13). Like the Good Thief they are already with Christ, living and acting close to him, with him and in him. There is a communion between them and ourselves, a fruitful communication. We can all have some idea of how much our Christian life and our awareness of the demands of faith owe to the influence of one or other of these great figures of the past. Some of them such as St. Paul, St. Augustine, St. Francis of Assisi, Brother Laurence of the Resurrection, St. Thérèse of Lisieux, are so present amongst us, active and real like our nearest friends and mentors—this is not a confession, I am mentioning them by chance although perhaps my historian's reflexes have led me to mention them in chronological order! But in addition to this influence, which is in some sort measurable, how much more important and efficacious, historically speaking (in the most secret and also in the most profound sense of the word) was and is and will always be the influence exercised by their intercession? I do not mean to attach undue value to minor devotions, but it is necessary to emphasize, in passing, the importance of an essential aspect of our faith that is often neglected. This is a doctrine that is far better authenticated than that of the hidden saints of the cabala or of Sufism and it weaves an even closer bond between the time that is lived in earthly history and that which is already in the eternal beyond of that history.[23]

22. *INCHOATIVE ESCHATOLOGY*

But this is not the time and place to linger over this particular aspect of the question, for we have not yet gone far enough with our analysis of the eschatological character of the time in which history takes place. We need to have a very clear realization of the subtle shades of meaning and the particular fervor with which Christians pronounce—or should pronounce—the words of the third request of the Our Father: "Thy Kingdom come." We are no longer living in the time of the Old Covenant in which this prayer, whether explicitly formulated or not, is to be found on almost every page of the Prophets' writings; for them it was simply the expression of their longing for the Kingdom of the future. It was pure expectancy. Nor are we living still amongst those disciples who had the privilege

[23] Cf. Jacques Maritain, *A propos de l'Eglise du ciel*, in Nova et Vetera, 1964, pp. 205–228.

of accompanying the Lord on his way on this earth. Remember the image of the triptych: the time we are living in, the time of the Church, corresponds to the third panel of the triptych portraying the divine economy, the plan for the salvation of humanity. We are (by which, of course, I mean, we have to be, we should be, we try to become) the saints of the end time, of the Last Day. These expressions are repeatedly used in the New Testament, reiterating and renewing the words of the Prophets (Ac 2:17; He 1:2; I P 1:20, etc.). Also, we cannot ignore the impassioned discussions that have been going on ever since the beginning of this century concerning the correct interpretation of the New Testament eschatology. It is not necessary to restate or summarize these discussions here; it will be sufficient for me to outline my own position. First of all it is perhaps redundant to say that I completely disagree with J. Weiss, A. Schweitzer and M. Werner when they speak of "consequent eschatology," which means that they believe Jesus and his disciples to have held an erroneous illusory belief in the imminent triumph of the kingdom. Similarly I cannot agree with R. Bultmann and his "existential eschatology" which, even if this is not intended, does in fact destroy the essential reality of the overall history of humanity. Some formulations of the question are more satisfactory, but I still cannot agree to speak, with C. H. Dodd, of "fulfilled eschatology" (even if one is speaking only of the ministry of our Lord, Jesus Christ), for it seems to me that this is already saying too much, nor can I speak only of "anticipated eschatology," with O. Cullmann for, as I understand it, this does not say enough. Should we use the expression D. Mollat uses, of an eschatology that has "begun"? This seems to come closer to what we are looking for, but the term is a little too static, perhaps. I would prefer to speak, with G. Florovsky, of the eschatology that has been "inaugurated" or, better still, with E. Haenchen and J. Jeremias, of an eschatology that is in the midst of being accomplished: "inchoative eschatology." The word is perhaps a little pedantic, but it is the word that St. Augustine himself used (*Enarr. in Ps* 64:4; see Cassian, *Conl.* IX, 19).

The fact that the time after Christ in which we live is not moved only by the thrust toward the future, toward what is to come, is of great importance. It is, of course, a time of hope, the time of the *Marana tha*, the *"Come, Lord,"* and it is true that St. Paul wrote, as though in passing, "our salvation is not in sight, we should not have to be hoping for it if it were" (Rm 8:24), but there is nothing more dangerous than to concentrate feverishly on one verse of Scripture as though it eliminated all others. It is always important to take into consideration what is vouched for by the whole of revelation, and in this instance it would be rash to forget that, just a few pages before, in the same letter, St. Paul corrected himself in advance, as it were, and spoke of salvation as already won (Rm 5:1: "Through our Lord Jesus Christ, by faith we are judged righteous and at peace with God"), seeing hope as standing in relation to a grace in which we are already firmly established.

St. Paul does not hesitate to make liberal use of the art of antithetical rhetoric, and Augustine also uses it later, in his attempt to express the paradoxical tension which is the characteristic sign of the time of the Church, the time of our history. And not only St. Paul; St. John also speaks in the same vein in his first Epistle: "We are already the children of God but what we are to be in the future has not yet been revealed" (I Jn 3:2). The exegetes are all in agreement, moreover, when they stress the striking fact that the Evangelists all speak of the Kingdom of God sometimes as an event in the future for which we are waiting and sometimes as a mystery that is already present "amongst us, within us" (the phrase in Lk 17:21 is recognized as being ambiguous).

And so, while we must not lose a sense of the historical eschatology that we are still waiting for, in hope and expectation, it is very important to maintain a very lively sense of that mysterious intertwining of the future and the "already-here," the present and the "not-yet." The images and types used in the inspired texts to suggest the meaning of the spiritual history of mankind are all dynamic: the increasing number of saints and the gradual progress toward the full complement, the construction of the City or of the Temple, the growth of the Body of Christ. These images help us to avoid a notion of the time of the Church that would be too passive, as though it were simply a period of waiting and hope; on the contrary, it implies a positive activity, a realization, still inchoative as we have seen, but already inherent in being, a part of the final being which will reach its consummation and consecration at the eschaton.

The time in which we are living is already, properly speaking, a messianic time. The pouring out of the Spirit that was promised by the Prophets (Jl 2:28f = Ac 2:16–21) began at Pentecost. Yes, the Spirit never ceases to pour himself out on his "sons and daughters" under our very eyes, although most of the time he does so in mysterious ways. This is why the notion, so dear to St. Irenaeus, of a gradual "habit" that humanity acquires, enabling it to receive the Holy Spirit, seems to me to be of such deep significance. He uses this idea both in respect to the Old Covenant: God sent his prophets to "accustom men dwelling on earth to bear his Spirit" (IV, 14, 2M; 21, 3) and in respect to the Incarnation: "This Spirit also came down on the Son of God who had become Son of man, accustoming himself, by dwelling in him, to dwell in the human race" (III, 17, 1). In the same way, "in the end-time," the time that was inaugurated at Pentecost, the Lord accustoms us little by little to treasure the Spirit of the Father within ourselves, to bear Life within us (IV, 38, 1; V, 3, 3). We must keep a firm hold on both ends of the line, both aspects of the paradoxical mystery of the time of the Church: the notion of inchoation, of a progressive development already begun, makes it possible for us to understand that, while it is perfectly real, yet its messianic character is still in a state of becoming.

It is significant—and, quite certainly, one of the tangible signs of the pouring out of the Spirit—that a voice was raised very early on in the last Council, to denounce the sin of "triumphalism" for which Catholics have such a penchant. A very long time ago the Spirit warned the Church against those who claimed that "the resurrection has already taken place" (2 Tm 2:18). Triumphalism springs from the fact that the militant Church forgets, or attempts to forget, that she is still a pilgrim Church. It is a very dangerous tendency and source of an almost purely verbal satisfaction which causes us to close our eyes to our real responsibilities and to the most exacting and immediate demands of our vocation as Christians.

Oh no! we are not yet risen from the dead. What we shall be, what we must be, is not yet apparent in the light of day. The victory that Christ has won has not yet borne all its visible fruits. "At present, it is true, we are not able to see that everything has been put under his command" (He 2:8). As we have already said, the time of the Church is the time of faith in which we make our way through a mysterious twilight, seeing darkly as in a mirror. We shall not be unfaithful to the spirit of St. Augustine if we venture to liken this time to a Lenten period, which should be one of penance and conversion. We must accept and face up squarely to all the frustration, pain and hardship which this implies, trials coming from within as well as from without.

From within, to begin with: here we must recapitulate what we have already said about the ambivalence of historical time and apply it now to the time that is lived personally by the individual Christian. It is the time of the call to conversion, but conversion is always incomplete and always needs to be undertaken afresh. It is a time spent in lukewarmness and infidelity to our lofty vocation. As we well know, it is the time during which sin still holds sway over us, and this very often in spite of what we really want or claim to want. Seen collectively, sin disfigures the glorious beauty of the King's Betrothed, it rends and soils the seamless robe which should be so beautiful in its universality and diversity (Ps 45:14–15). This is the time in which scandal, heresy and schisms bruise the face of the Church and prevent her from being altogether without "speck or wrinkle or anything like that, but holy and faultless" (Ep 5:27).

But if there are perils from within there are also perils from without: this is the period of trials and contradictions, of persecution of all kinds. It is our time of constancy (this is a key-word in the New Testament ethic in a far deeper sense than it ever was with the Stoics), of heroic fidelity—in a word: of martyrdom (*De catech. rud.*, 24, 44). We have to stress this repeatedly, for the ingenuous optimism of the modern notion of progress constantly threatens to contaminate and emasculate our theology of history. The Lord never promised his Church a peaceful life illuminated by the reflected glory of eternal beatitude. On the contrary, he promised a time of hardship in which those who put us to death would think they were "doing a holy duty for God" (Jn 16:2). We cannot speak of triumph until the Day of Judgment. Only then will the pagans cease to speak ill of the work of the saints which has been hidden, or which has seemed ambiguous to them, until then, and glorify God for these wonderful works in the Day of his coming. (I P 2:12).

The ancients were distrustful of too much effortless happiness, because they feared the jealously of the gods. And we have something to learn both from the story of Polycrate's ring and from the words of the Apostle: "It is when people are saying, 'How quiet and peaceful it is' that the worst suddenly happens . . ." (1 Th 5:3). A Christian should be on his guard when things seem to be going too well for him and those close to him (for, alas! things never go too well for all men). We should learn to be far more exigent with regard to our apparent successes and be capable of appreciating their limits and their ambiguity and ambivalence.

Even now we only have to look at the Church's past to have some idea of how fragile and approximate are those moments in which the Church has seemed to triumph, in which the visible curve of history seems to follow and identify with the curve of the history of salvation, the true history of mankind. At best it is never more than tangential to it for one fleeting moment of time, like the impression of being united for one brief moment with the choirs of angels when singing the Sanctus (or the Cherubikon) during the liturgy. We know what actually became of the "Christian Empire," and so we should be in a position to gauge the tremendous illusions entertained by Eusebius Pamphili after the triumph of Constantine and the Council of Nicaea. We are in a position to know how many "Christian Emperors" formented heresy and persecuted their fellow men. All of them, without exception, showed themselves to be only too willing to turn the spirtual forces of the Church they claimed to serve to the service of their own will to power.

This brings us to one of the cases in which the ethic of the New

Covenant is in most direct contrast with the spirit of the Old, for in the Old Covenant it was generally considered that punishment was meted out during one's lifetime, and the Chosen People were sure that victory would be accorded to them in return for their fidelity. A reading of the Old Testament from a point of view that was too literal, not sufficiently historical and not in the perspective of the New Testament, had a disastrous influence on men's thought during the era of Christendom, especially in the area of political thought. There were all too many Christian sovereigns, from Constantine to Charlemagne or Louis XIV, who were willing to think of themselves as, and to allow themselves to be honored as, a new King David.

Once we have clearly seen and conceded all this, and are careful not to forget it, we are in a position to examine the messianic time of the third period of the history of Salvation. It is the time of grace, and this in the very precise sense in which St. Augustine, interpreting St. Paul, defines it by contrasting it on the one hand with the two phases that can be seen in the Old Testament—before the Law and under the Law—and on the other hand with the "beyond" of history and time, when we shall be in the state of eschatological peace (*Expos. quar. prop. Ep. ad Rom.*, 13:18).

The indwelling of grace in man is inchoative but real. This would be the moment to call to mind the theology of the sacraments, the hierarchical ministry and the institutional structure of the Church . . . but I see no necessity to emphasize this, as it is so self-evident. On the other hand we would still be within the heart of our subject if I should suggest that the reader meditate seriously on the invaluable notion that St. Paul throws out, almost in passing, of the "pledge" ("token" or "earnest") of the Spirit, the first-fruits of the inheritance to come. It is a notion that helps to bring out both the present reality and the inchoation of our participation in the divine life during this period of history that is destined to disappear with the coming of the eternal sabbath.

23. THE CHARACTERISTICS OF THE PRESENT TIME

We can now move on a step further in our search for the exact status of a Christian in this time of the Church. Our theology of history, like any theology that is not just empty ratiocination, should be the basis for a certain spirituality. What practical consequences flow from the fact that a Christian is conscious of his place in the history of salvation? How can he, and how should he, live this truth in his daily life?

To begin with we should stress a first duty which is completely self-evident but has often become utterly insipid in our traditionally Christian milieus: the primary characteristic note of the time of the Church is to be the time of the mission. It is the time of the New Covenant, the "year of favour from Yahweh" (Is 61:2) announced by the Prophet Isaiah—St. Irenaeus comments admirably on this text (II, 22, 1–2M). The time that lies between the first and the second Parousia, between the first and the second coming of the Lord, is the time in which God brings the saints, the fruits of history, to their full maturity. It is the time of God's patience (2 P 3:9; see 2 M 6:14), of God's mercy (*Enarr. in Ps* 32, 11, 1, 10); the time given to men to take advantage of the salvation that is held out to them, salvation which is in itself already won but which still must be grasped by men.

This is the time in which God wins a chosen people, the time of the "convocation": this is the correct meaning of the Hebrew word Qahal, translated into Greek as *ecclesia,* the Church. St. Augustine, although he knew very little Hebrew, was aware of the etymological origin of the word: . . . "convocation, whence comes the name of the Church" (*Enarr. in Ps* 81, 1). This is the time of the call: St. Paul likes to use the term "called to be saints" when he is speaking to the Christians (Rm. 1:7; I Co 1:2). We must try to go beyond the sclerosis of anti-Pelagian polemics and recapture the profound and lasting value of a notion that is an essential part of our faith, that of "predestination," the call that God addresses to those whom he has chosen and loved since before the world was made (Ep 1:4).

Yes, the time of the Church is the time that is needed for all God's children to assemble or, as St. John Chrysostom so delightfully put it, the time that is needed for all God's children to gather together around the sumptuous, well-furnished table of the father of the family (*In Spi. fidei*, III, 10, P.G. 51, 299). It is not difficult to see the practical conclusion that we can all draw from this; for God, who can do all things and who needs the help of no one, has yet asked us to be his "fellow workers" (I Th 3:2; I Co 3:9) working with and for him. The time of the Church appears then, first and foremost, as the time of the Kerygma, the time in which the Good News must be proclaimed. This being so, how can someone who has received the Good News do nothing about it? How can he help feeling the need to shout it from the rooftops, to proclaim it before all men so that they, his brothers, may share his happiness?

And so this is the time of evangelization, of the mission in the most immediate sense of the word. It was with this solemn command that our Lord left us, according to the last verses of St. Matthew's Gospel: "Go therefore, make disciples of all nations" (Mt 28:19). One could say a great deal about the clear conscience of the average Christian who relies on the specialized organizations and the professional "missionaries" to accomplish this duty for him, as though the "propagation of the faith" were not an immediate, daily and universal duty for all of us—as though he could shift the burden of his duty onto someone else. (I say this without in any way contesting the obvious necessity of "missionaries" in the traditional sense of the word.)

Our fathers in the faith did not see things this way: they saw the Church as being missionary by essence. If we want just one example I could mention that of Eusebius Pamphili, Bishop of

Caesarea, who wrote about the beginning of the second century in his *Ecclesiastical History*: "For in very truth numbers of the disciples of that day felt their souls smitten by the divine word with a more ardent passion for philosophy, and so at first fulfilled the Savior's command, by distributing their goods to the needy. Afterwards they set out on journeys from home and performed the work of evangelists, making it their aim to preach to such as had not yet heard the word of the faith at all, and to give them the book of the divine Gospels. But they were content to lay the foundations only of the faith in some foreign places, appointing others as pastors to whom they entrusted the care of those lately brought in; then they could depart to other lands and nations with the grace and cooperation of God . . ." (III, 37, 2–3).

And then again, one of the conclusions of the Gospel (this time Mark's Gospel, 16:17–18) is that the time of the mission is the time of miracles and of manifestations of the power of the Spirit. From my own experience I know this to be true: whenever the fire of missionary zeal bursts forth again in the Church the charismata of the first Pentecost can once again be seen on the earth—all those who lived through the early days of the mission to the workers, the worker-priests, the little brothers of Charles de Foucauld can bear me out in this . . .

But of all miracles the most brilliant, the most wonderful, is the miracle of holiness. As St. Augustine said, the time of the Church is the time of grace. It is when we see holiness that we are most vividly aware of the profoundly eschatological nature of the present in which we are living the third phase of the history of salvation—of an eschatology which is, I must repeat, only inchoative. When we meditate on the lives of the saints, the great contemplatives and mystics, we feel that in their most privileged moments they were granted an anticipated experience of the state we all hope for. The life they had attained was not of a different nature to the life that will be ours at the eschaton. One could even go so far as to say that—at least for the brief moment in which the weight of the flesh seemed to annihilate itself before bringing them abruptly back to earth—there was no longer any essential difference for them between their life in history and the blessed life beyond history.

Ancient oriental monasticism, which was fond of defining the the monk's ideal as a life akin to that of the angels, understood this perfectly. Of course, the comparison must be understood as a rhetorical image; to take it literally would be absurd (he who would act the angel acts the brute . . .) if not blasphemous. We are created as men, and it would be pointless to imagine that we can escape from the laws that the Creator has imposed on human nature. The Desert Fathers, those great professionals of asceticism, experts in spiritual experience, only spoke of a "certain similarity" or of "having a foretaste of the pledge of a heavenly dwelling" (Cassian, *Conl.* X, 7). They took very good care to keep in mind that even the greatest saint must continue to avoid the snares of fallen nature and of sin.

What is meant is simply that, to the exact degree in which the contemplative man has managed by asceticism to gain control over the dark powers of the flesh, and to the extent to which he has received the grace to do so, the life he is endeavoring to live on earth is already, quite literally, an anticipation, a foretaste and a beginning of eternal life. What is it he is trying to put into practice—if he is not shackled by his earthly mission—if not life as he hopes to know it one day, the life that will consist, and already consists, in loving God and praying to him ceaselessly?

Indeed, another favorite theme of monastic tradition is that the prayer of a Christian on earth is linked to the cosmic liturgy eternally celebrated by the angels in heaven. If this is true in a high degree for the monk, the contemplative and the mystic it is also true, on the ontological level, for all Christians. The difference is only one of degree and practice. For, after all, what must a Christian do if not love God with all his heart and all his soul and, as far as he is able, "pray constantly" (I Th 5:17; this precept must surely apply to everyone)?

It is hardly necessary to say that this spirituality is in radical contradiction to a certain attitude which claims to be "eschatological" but which has not, and has never had, anything more than a purely polemical existence in an authentic, healthy Christianity. This attitude consists in seeing history as a time during which faith only serves to keep hope alive, a time of purely passive waiting. No indeed, this time is filled with activity, and the old translations of Ephesians 5:16 read: "Redeem our times for our times are evil" (we have since learned that both here and in Col. 4:5 the phrase would be better rendered by: "make the best use of your time" or "use every occasion to the full"). This is the time, "as long as the day lasts" (Jn 9:4) in which we have to accomplish the works of light, while the sun of justice enlightens us. And progressively we discover that this liturgical service has its place amongst the most clearly defined works of light.

24. A ROYAL PRIESTHOOD

I must make it clear that the term "liturgical service" is to be taken in the sense of its deeper implication. The lessons of monastic spirituality which we have just mentioned, however valuable and enlightening they may be in themselves, could mislead the reader and cause him to limit his reflection to the question of personal sanctification. (Especially if he forgets to what extent the spirituality of the desert was concerned, over and above the monk's personal growth in sanctity, with the burden of intercession for all men and for the whole world.) The community aspect is always inseparable from the personal aspect. The love of God is closely bound up with the love of neighbor, and the liturgical function is, by its very nature, ordered precisely to the love of our fellow man. The time of the Church is a time of prayer and intercession.

At this point I would like to allude to *The Martyrdom of St. Polycarp*: when the Roman police came to arrest him and take him away to be martyred the old Bishop of Smyrna begged for an hour to pray as he wanted. In his prayer he remembered "all that ever had dealings with him, great and small, well-known and unknown, and the whole Catholic Church throughout the world . . ." (7, 2–8, 1).

Our generation has rediscovered the worth of this great fundamental dogma of the royal priesthood of the faithful which had been obscured for far too long in the practical spirituality of Catholicism by a preoccupation with anti-Protestant polemics and apologetics, as though the "so-called priesthood of the faithful" were a threat to the hierarchical and sacramental priesthood. The poverty of the Latin vocabulary also contributed to this state of affairs: the word "priest" is used to translate both *iereus* and *presbyteros* and the word "sacerdocy" is used sometimes with reference to the sovereign high priest, Mediator of the New Covenant who has entered the heavenly sanctuary once and for all, having redeemed us with his own blood (He 9:11–12), and sometimes with reference to the ministerial function of the hierarchical, sacramental priesthood given by the sacrament of Orders and derived from the sovereign high priest. This latter priesthood—the ecclesiastical function through which an immediate contact is established and maintained, throughout the succeeding generations and over the whole face of the earth, with the unique mediator, source of all grace—certainly has an essential role to play in our Christian life, but it is of another order to the priesthood of the unique high priest.

The majority of the members of the Church participate in the priesthood of Christ on quite another level and in the measure in which each one is incorporated in Christ. The most widely favored image of the "body of Christ" makes it possible to express precisely this unity: the head and the members are one and thus make up the fullness of Christ (Ep 1:23), or "the whole Christ," as St. Augustine translated it.

The fact that the time of the Church as it is, or should be, lived by Christians is first and foremost a liturgical time is crystal clear through the most explicit revelation. The solemn promise of the Old

Law, "I will count you a kingdom of priests, a consecrated nation" (Ex 19:6; see also Is 61:6), was of course already fulfilled, for the first time, in the history of Israel, the chosen people. But this was a prophetic realization in the sense that it was both a first fulfillment and the announcement of a more perfect fulfillment still to come. And now, if we compare the clear-cut phrase of the Book of Revelation, he has "made us a line of kings, priests to serve his God and Father" (Rv 1:6 and 5:10), with the original Old Testament verse from which it comes, we can see that it is a clear declaration that the time of the promise has now begun, that it is no longer only in the future. Or again we can find the same declaration, in a context that is particularly enlightening, in St. Peter's First Epistle (2:9). Gathering all the different messianic traits in one phrase he declares that the promise has now been fulfilled: "but you are a chosen race (Is 43:20), a royal priesthood, a consecrated nation (Ex 19:6; Dt 7:6), a people set apart" (Is 43:21). And so, in the Church and from the beginning of the time of the Church, the eschatological promises are already inchoatively fulfilled, they are in the process of being accomplished. St. Augustine—and tradition has followed his thought in this matter—has shown that the well-known passage of Revelation (20:1-6) should be interpreted in this perspective. This is the passage that conjures up the picture of a first resurrection in which the just are restored to life and reign for a thousand years, with Christ. It is a text full of mystery, and the generations before Augustine had dwelt on it at length and heavily embroidered on it. It must be understood as referring simply to the saints and to the Church which is already the kingdom of Christ, the kingdom of heaven—at least for those sons of the Church who already, as far as this is possible within the human condition, lead the life that will one day be theirs in heaven (*City of God* XX, 9, 1 quoting Col 3:1-2 and Ph 3:20).

At this stage we might elaborate on the implications of such an incorporation in Christ, the sovereign high priest, the participation which unites us to him to the point of uniting us in redemptive suffering. One cannot forget the overwhelming significance of St.

Paul's "It makes me happy to suffer for you, as I am suffering now, and in my own body to do what I can to make up all that has still to be undergone by Christ for the sake of his body, the Church" (Col 1:24). But we cannot discuss everything, and we must restrict ourselves to that which sheds some light on the Christian's mode of participation in the history of salvation.

God asks that by living holy lives and by prayer, we wait for and *hasten* the Day of his coming (2 P 3:12). We have received the good news and the education in Christ that is given by the teaching of the Church and the participation in the grace of the sacraments. We know what "a pure offering" and "the sacrifice of the spirit" mean. We should, therefore, see ourselves as the holy class, the priestly people, with the responsibility of prayer and of continuing the worship of God; in a word, charged with the special task of sanctifying the human race as it makes its way through the dimension of time, just as the priests and Levites were the sanctifiers of the people of Israel during their long march through the desert. Following St. Paul's example we all should be "as a priest of Jesus Christ, and I am to carry out my priestly duty by bringing the Good News from God to the pagans and so make them acceptable as an offering, made holy by the Holy Spirit" (Rm 15:16). It is up to us to ensure that the historical work accompilshed by all men be transformed into an "acceptable offering."

25. THE SALT OF THE EARTH

We have to try, here, to restore the fecundity of a doctrine, very rich in content, which inspired the lives of the early generation of Christians, although it was largely obliterated during the centuries of Christendom, when sociologically speaking the whole population was made up of members, or so-called members, of the Church. The sacerdotal function—by which I still mean the participation of all the faithful in the unique priesthood of Christ, not the ministerial function—tended to be less in evidence for lack of any exterior sign to distinguish those who exercised the function from those in favor of whom it was exercised.

In contrast to this, during the first centuries, as long as the Roman Empire was at least potentially the persecutor and the Christians only a small minority whose existence in a civilization hostile to, or at least ignorant of, their faith was always threatened, the duties which bound them to the whole of mankind were naturally in the forefront of their minds. Elsewhere[24] I have had occasion to collect the patristic documents which treat of this theme, from Justin to Origen and beyond. I will limit myself here to reproducing a page, deservedly well-known, in which that deep conviction is expressed with particular clarity:

For Christians are not distinguished from the rest of mankind either in locality or in speech or in customs. For they dwell not somewhere in cities of their own, neither do they use some different language, nor practise an extraordinary kind of life. Nor again do they possess any invention discovered by any intelligence or study of ingenious men, nor are they masters of any human dogma as some are. But while they dwell in cities of Greeks and barbarians as the lot of each is cast, and follow the native customs in dress and food and other arrangements of life, yet the constitution of their own citizenship, which they set forth, is marvellous, and confessedly contradicts expectation. . . . In a word, what the soul is in a body, this the Christians are in the world. The soul is spread through all the members of the body, and Christians through the divers cities of the world. The soul hath its abode in the body, and yet it is not of the body. So Christians have their abode in the world, and yet they are not of the world. The soul, which is invisible, is guarded in the body, which is visible: so Christians are recognized as being in the world, and yet their religion remaineth invisible. The flesh hateth the soul and wageth war with it, though it receiveth no wrong, because it

[24] See my commentary of *Epistle to Diognetus*, French edition, collection Sources chrétiennes, Paris, 1965, p. 129–176.

is forbidden to indulge in pleasures; so the world hateth Christians, though it receiveth no wrong from them, because they set themselves against its pleasures. The soul loveth the flesh which hateth it, and the members: so Christians love those that hate them. The soul is enclosed in the body, and yet itself holdeth the body together; so Christians are kept in the world as in a prison-house, and yet they themselves hold the world together. The soul, though itself immortal, dwelleth in a mortal tabernacle; so Christians sojourn amidst perishable things, while they look for the imperishability which is in the heavens. (*Epistle to Diognetus* 5:1–3; 6:1–8).

The anonymous Apologist who wrote this letter to Diognetus—apparently in Alexandria about the year 200—did no more than express, in very beautiful Greek and with a particularly delightful turn of phrase, just what the Fathers repeatedly said both before and after him.

A moment's thought makes it evident that he was simply expressing the content of the formal teaching of the Gospel: it is in the Sermon on the Mount that we can read those awe-inspiring words: "You are the salt of the earth . . . you are the light of the world . . ." (Mt 5:13–16). We cannot slide out from under this responsibility. The impassioned words of the Book of Isaiah do not apply only to the eschatological Jerusalem: "Arise, shine out, for your light has come, the glory of Yahweh is rising on you, though night still covers the earth and darkness the peoples . . ." Is (60:1–2). I repeat, the Kingdom has already begun, Christ already reigns in us. St. Matthew's Gospel stresses the apostolic obligation that flows from this: "You are the light of the world. A city built on a hill-top cannot be hidden. No one lights a lamp to put it under a tub; they put it on the lampstand where it shines for everyone in the house. In the same way your light must shine in the sight of men . . ." (Mt 5:14–16).

A faithful Christian must accept all the teaching that flows from the inspired word wherever it may be found in Scripture and the sense of this passage from Matthew can be much better understood when read in relation to the Gospel of John in which Jesus says of himself: "I am the light of the world; anyone who follows me will not be walking in the dark; he will have the light of life" (Jn 8:12). To the extent to which, incorporated in Christ, we are part of the whole Christ, to the extent to which we are one with him in a mysterious but deeply real way, it is possible for us to become what we are, what we are meant to be (for this notion is not simply a description, it is a norm): the "light of the world."

And similarly we are, we must be, the "salt of the earth." But if salt becomes tasteless, what can make it salty again? It is good for nothing, and can only be thrown out to be trampled underfoot by men" (Mt 5:13). Nurtured by constant familiarity with the Old Testament, the Fathers had no difficulty in understanding the full import of this image, and certainly they made the most of the implications of the common use of salt: seasoning and salting for preserving foods. The presence of Christians in the world should give it flavor (is it necessary to insist that this flavor will only be perceptible to God?) and, on the other hand, it should prevent humanity, including sinners, from crumbling away completely in corruption (see St. Augustine: *Sermon on the Mount,* I, 6 [13–14]).

This, too, is only true, strictly speaking, with relation to the Judgment of God, and yet are we not already in a position to measure the extent to which corruption is growing and spreading in our Western civilization in proportion to the breakdown and gradual foundering of the Christian heritage which, however imperfectly, had tried to mark the structures and the mentality of this civilization with the spirit of the Gospel? The neo-paganism of our contemporaries does not strike a very joyful note. These unfortunate men boast of having eliminated "the infamous Christian notion of sin," and the very notion of man is turning to dust in their hands, now that they can rejoice at having already lost the notion of God!

But the primary and most profound significance (as the parallel text in Mk 9:49–50 suggests) of the image of "the salt of the earth" is of a liturgical nature. It refers, implicitly, to the ritual prescription of the old Law: "You must salt every oblation that you offer, and you must never fail to put on your oblation the salt of the Covenant

with your God: to every offering you are to join an offering of salt
to Yahweh your God" (Lv 2:13; see also Nb 18:19; Ezk 43:24). Yes
indeed! The earth, the world, humanity, history, can only become the
"acceptable offering" if they are salted with the Christian salt. This
is not a play on words. It is a question of getting back to the profound significance of the historical responsibility of the Christian
in all its awe-inspiring simplicity.

26. THE DUTIES OF A MINORITY

The testimony of history is there to bear us out: the Christians of
the first two or three centuries assumed this responsibility fully, in
all awareness and confidence, humility and determination. And yet
they were a small, despised minority. They should be a model and
encouragement to us. While the thin veneer of a residual Christianization, which blinded our predecessors for so long to the real state
of the modern world, is flaking away, we have abruptly woken up to
the fact that we are no more than a tiny minority in a world that is
still pagan, or which has become pagan all over again—a minority
that is no more than tolerated with irritable or scornful indulgence
here, actively persecuted elsewhere. It is not always a very comfortable position to be in personally, but above all we must stress
that it is in itself a painful, conflict-ridden situation: we cannot help
being distressed at being such a weak minority within the social
body, weak both in numbers and through our own mediocrity. This
alone should be enough to revive our missionary vocation. When we
see such a wealth of human gifts among the pagans, so much natural
virtue, such a capacity for self-giving, we can only think: how
much more worthy they are than we to bear the message of Christ,
what great potential they have for sanctity!

But shall the clay say to the potter: Why did you make me like this? We must fight the battles of Christ wherever he has placed us in history. Wherever we may be and whatever we may be, we still have the same priestly responsibility toward the whole world. It is up to us to pray in the name of all men, our brothers, and to offer to God the offering of the whole of their history.

It must be quite obvious that we do not consider ourselves as a sort of privileged aristocracy on the spiritual level. How could anyone who is aware of his own mediocrity and unworthiness in face of the staggering task that has been allotted to him, entertain any such idea? We all know too well that, except for the saints, we are very poor priests. . . .

The confidence, the bold trust that springs from faith—in this context we might examine the content of the Pauline notion of *parresia* (Ep 3:12 etc.)—can never give rise to self-sufficiency and pride in the heart of a believer. We know only too well that we "are only the earthenware jars that hold this treasure" (2 Co 4:7). To the extent to which we gain a better understanding of the glory of the message that we have received and that we must pass on, we shall the more keenly feel our unworthiness. Can it be possible that we react by sin and, what is worse, by mediocrity, to such a high calling and such promises? Ah, if only we would take heed of the warning sent by the Spirit to the Church of Laodicea: "You are neither cold nor hot. I wish you were one or the other, but since you are neither but only lukewarm, I will spit you out of my mouth" (Rv 3:15–16). It is not we who possess the truth, it is truth that possesses us, that should possess us entirely. But the truth is entangled with our sluggishness and the practical refusal which, scandalously, accompanies our theoretical acceptance of the faith. There is nothing here to be especially proud or reassured about. We know, from the mouth of our Lord himself, that on the Day of Judgment more mercy will be shown to Sodom and Gomorrha than to us who have heard the word of God and who have not listened to it (Mt 10:15 and parallel).

Such are the foundations of our theology of history, such is our faith, such is our hope. They are built not on the conjectures and

dreams of human thought (*Ep. to Diogn.* 5, 3) but on the rock of
the revelation, that is on the very word of God, which lives forever
in his Church and which we have received through the Church.
This is the origin and foundation of our security and our strength,
and it is what makes it possible for us to move resolutely toward an
encounter with the modern world and all its ambiguities. As we
mentioned in the beginning, we see pagans today alternately adopt-
ing one of two contradictory solutions to the problem of history.
There are those, ranging from Kantians to Marxists, who believe
that they know what history is or should be. It is true that the subtler
minds no longer profess the ingenuous beliefs of the early phases
of Positivism, when Comte wrote: "The doctrine that can give an
adequate explanation of the past as a whole will, by the very fact
of that feat, inevitably win mental control over the future." Indeed
the whole of history known to man can be recapitulated in the space
of fifteen minutes in view of a bid for the future. Every human
action, every forward-looking plan, unless it is purely utopian and
has no connection with history, must necessarily be accompanied by
a retrospective view. The man of action, if he wants to be in the
mainstream of reality, will always try to build the future on what
has been acquired in the past. But we must not be taken in by the
undertaking whose success is assured in advance and which is thereby worthless.

This has become perfectly evident at least for the most reasonable
amongst our contemporaries—there will always be some fanatics and
some simpletons. They grant that all philosophy of history is a
"practical idea" in the Kantian sense of the word, an hypothesis, an
ideal, an inspiration and guide for the action that is planned—in
other words, a hope. But then the most obstinately rational part of
us cannot help saying, Who says so? What assurance do we have
that this new project, however seductive it may be, will meet with
success in contrast to so many others, no less attractive in their day,
conceived by other men of other times—undertakings of which we
can still see the vestiges in the cemeteries of history? Kant, to stick
to the one example, saw humanity as moving toward a universal

cosmopolitan state which would free men from war. This was a noble ideal and it could well serve as a guide for action in the attempt to make it come true. But who can guarantee that it will be fulfilled one day? Who can tell whether the United Nations is not already as complete a failure as the defunct League of Nations? There was something very pathetic in the encouragements that Paul VI lavished on this organization in his speech of October, 1965 . . . Our only assurance is in God's promise.

On the other side we meet people who hope for nothing further from man nor, consequently, from history. They resign themselves to analyzing man's finiteness. And yet they, too, know very well that within the hidden depths of the finiteness of man there is an opening, a beginning and, as it were, a visceral summons to move forward, beyond his own limits. Man is a finite being, but he is also a creature who has a capacity for the absolute. To those who have hope for man, we must preach faith—we must tell them not to lean on man, who is a broken reed, but to hold on only to the word of God—and to those who have no hope we must preach hope. Their question is: Who can guarantee that the inner depths will ever be filled by being, that man's hunger and thirst for the absolute can ever be satisfied? To these people we should present ourselves as the heralds of good news, the good news which man was not expecting but which the Incarnate Word came to bring and to guarantee. And then the experience of our finiteness becomes like the hollow mold into which our promised fulfillment, the divinization for which we are waiting, can be poured: "I have noticed limitations to all (human, earthly) perfection, but (you have taught me, O Lord, that) your commandment has no limit at all" (Ps 119:96).

PART TWO

27. PRAY FOR THE COMING

Now that we have recapitulated and, as far as possible consciously assumed the doctrinal foundations of this theology of history in our own minds, it is time to move on from the theory to the *praxis* and to ask ourselves in all seriousness what manner of men we must be to live "holy and saintly lives while you wait and long for the Day of God to come"—to stick to the terms St. Peter uses in his Second Epistle (3:11 f). As I said earlier in commenting on this text, such a theology does not lead to passiveness; it implies a whole spirituality of action.

Anyone who has really understood that the essential thing being accomplished through the medium of human temporality, the true meaning of history, is the filling up of the ranks of the people of saints, the building of the blessed City, the growth of the Body of Christ . . . anyone who has understood this cannot avoid asking himself the question, urgent, sometimes, to the point of anguish: What can I do to hasten the coming of the Kingdom? The first answer that comes to mind, because it is so obvious—and it will always have a position of priority—is suggested by the preceding verse in the same letter: "Pray." We must pray without ceasing, since this is what we have been told to do, and we have been told to do so, precisely with a view to hastening the coming of the Kingdom: "Thy Kingdom come."

Perhaps we should note in passing that although we speak, following the inspired author, of "hastening the Parousia," it is obvious that it is only in a metaphorical sense that we can speak of doing violence to God and imposing our will on him (if this has any meaning, even, that would not be blasphemous). God is the unique Lord of History, and the economy of salvation will be accomplished in the way he has willed it in his providence and wisdom: "How deep his wisdom and knowledge—and how impossible to penetrate his motives or understand his methods" (Rm 11:33). Yet he has given us a commandment which endures, and he cannot have given it to us for nothing: our prayer, our obedience, our action, also have a place in the overall plan of collective salvation if we may be permitted to express the traditional notion of *oikonomia* in this way.

To pray implies also, with the grace of God, to be converted in the fullest sense of the words *metanoia, epistrophe,* to "turn back," to renew oneself, to become docile again to the action of grace and thereby to be purified and to grow in holiness, united with the sufferings and the redemptive work of Christ. This is the first rule for action which we can formulate, and it must be admitted that it is the specifically Christian way of life. It is normally realized through a concrete participation in the daily, collective life of the Church—the sacraments, the liturgy, all the Church's specifically religious work—and, as we have seen, missionary work has an essential part in this and will be accomplished in many different ways, beginning with the permanent witness of a Christian life.

We must proclaim it firmly and with faith: this is the first mode of historical action. The effectiveness of this mode of action is necessarily beyond the reach of our observation and even of our conjecture, but this does not give us the right to doubt that it is efficacious. The prayer of a holy man can have a far more profound and more immediately real influence than any of the flashy manifestations of visible history, simply because God has chosen to integrate this prayer into the chain of secondary causes. But I wonder whether it is true that this can only be seen with the eyes of faith?

Surely, even our experience shows us, at least by analogy, that it could be so. Does anyone deny the reality and depth of the specifically historical action, the tremendous influence on the behavior of so many of their brothers, of such spiritual souls as Thérèse of Lisieux and Charles de Foucauld, to mention only two recent examples from the annals of our Church. And yet they lived hidden lives and, insofar as they attempted to accomplish some visible work, they failed. But even apart from the role of intercessors they certainly played, which is beyond our range of vision, could anyone venture to estimate how far-reaching was the effect of their spiritual action?

This is the theme of the parable invented by R. H. Benson in a story that struck the imagination of Teilhard de Chardin most forcefully. I can still hear him talking about it, with such ardor, and he mentions it in *The Divine Milieu:* "In one of his stories, Robert Hugh Benson tells of a 'visionary' coming on a lonely chapel where a nun is praying. He enters. All at once he sees the whole world bound up and moving and organizing itself around that out-of-the-way spot, in tune with the intensity and inflection of the desires of that puny, praying figure.[25]

Contemplatives, whose vocation sets them on a course directly aimed at what is essential, will quite naturally dedicate themselves wholly to this type of historical action whose fecundity is still very largely a mystery to us. But I should add immediately that every Christian, even one who is most deeply immersed in the things of this world, also takes part in this action with some part of himself, the best part of himself. It is a mistake to put the two types of Martha and Mary, the active and the contemplative lives, into direct opposition. The constant teaching of the Fathers is that the one cannot exist without the other, especially the first cannot exist without the second. They exist for each other.

It is not easy to ensure the lasting health of a temporal undertaking. If, as we shall see, the problem is to ensure that it leads beyond itself, it is necessary to intersperse it with periods of silence and recollection during which one tries to regain a firmer footing in

[25] Teilhard de Chardin, *The Divine Milieu,* N.Y., Harper and Row, 1960.

the world of the spirit in order to start afresh, the spirit replenished
with light, the whole man endowed with greater strength. There
is far more wisdom than Renan liked to admit in his tale of the old
Sulpician who was so concerned by the fact that political undertakings were led by men who, quite obviously, did not practice
mental prayer!

28. *FAITH AND* RELIGION

All of that is self-evident. However, I feel that it has been just as
well to restate it and to do so in somewhat ingenuous terms—which
will seem outdated to many—in the first place because it is true and
primordial and in the second place because I feel that I must react
against the tendency that is already sufficiently prevalent all round
us of holding—in the manner of Dietrich Bonhoeffer—that a certain type of radical criticism of "religion" and its traditional forms
is a phase that must necessarily be gone through before we can
really renew the faith. Of course I do not want simply to reject this
movement whose deliberately paradoxical formulation expresses an
ambiguity resulting from a complex motivation rather than from a
dogmatic self-assurance.

On the one hand I can perfectly well understand the missionary
concern that sparks such a conviction. It is only too true and obvious
that the visible Church is made up of more sinners than saints. And
the result is that the sociological group of those who are Christians
in name only, presents a very tarnished image of the Church to
pagans who look at it from the outside and this is the principal
obstacle to the diffusion of the message that has to be handed on.
"No one has ever seen God" (I Jn 4:12). And so our fellow men
can only know whatever radiance and dimmed splendor is reflected
by our own faces. The same is true of the poverty of our language:
it has never been easy to speak of God in human language, and

yet we must speak of him. And today our words seem to have been devalued: "God," "Christianity," "Church" . . . as often as not these words conjure up such a caricature of the reality in the language of those who are not believers that one hesitates to use them openly. And so "the death of God" seems to many to be less a blasphemy than a necessary phase in a rejuvenated presentation of the Christian message to the neo-pagans of our times.

But a dialectic must not become a ruse. We cannot dwell for ever on something that should be no more than the first step in a process of rediscovery. Sooner or later we are going to have to face up to the fact that the scandal of the Cross contains elements that are absolutely unacceptable to human reason: "The language of the cross may be illogical to those who are not on the way to salvation, but those of us who are on the way see it as God's power to save" (I Co 1:18). We might with advantage reread the speech on the Areopagus, prototype of the pre-catechetical instruction of pagans. St. Paul goes as far as he can in his attempt to meet his audience on their own ground. Although "his whole soul was revolted at the sight of a city given over to idolatry" (Ac 17:16) he takes this as his own point of departure with a truly friendly understanding: "Men of Athens, I have seen for myself how scrupulous you are in all religious matters . . ." (17:23). But sooner or later he has to speak of some specific doctrine, and as soon as he utters the technical term for "rising from the dead," "some of them burst out laughing; others said, 'We would like to hear you talk about this again,'" (17:32).

In the second place I also recognize that just as we must continually meditate on the great dignity of Christianity and the unworthiness of Christians, we must also continually purify the inevitably inadequate image we have of God and free it—and this, too, is a dialectical movement—from the insidious infiltrations of a multiform anthropomorphism. (Psychoanalysis has taught us that this goes much deeper than simply imagining spiritual realities under corporeal forms; we must not project onto our image of God our own complexes and fantasies.) There is a permanent danger of substituting our own illusion for God and, in his name, calling on an empty phantom. A vain phantasm, my own error: Augustine uses these terms in the *Confessions* when he tells of the episode in his life when he lost a very dear friend (have not most of us gone through some such sorrow in our twenties?): "And if I said (to my soul), Trust in God, she very rightly obeyed me not; because that most dear friend, whom she had lost, was, being man, both truer and better than that phantasm she was bid to trust in" (*Confessions*, IV, 4 [9]; 7 [12]: one of the services rendered by history is that of saving modern man from the vain pride of thinking that his difficulties are quite new).

In the same way we must constantly work to purify our religious life and bring it "up to date," ridding it of forms that have been emptied of all content by the wear of the centuries and correcting the deviations which could make it simply the caricature of what it claims to be—the old self-centered magical practices which threaten to take the place of that true adoration in spirit and in truth which Christ, and the Prophets before him, proclaimed as the religion of the New Covenant. True! but just as the deep metaphysical intuitions of negative theology suppose and do not annihilate the truths posited by verbigerating theology, so this effort to disengage and purify our religious life, far from estranging us from the visible Church, will bring us back to it and its institutions and, above all, to its liturgy—in other words to the true "religion" that we cannot meaningfully oppose to faith.

29. *CITIZENS OF HEAVEN AND EARTH*

Even if the reader agrees with me in this, he has every right to be surprised by the fact that, so far, we have hardly mentioned what we usually understand by "human history" or, to put it in theological terms, the temporal order, our participation in the work and the battles of the earthly city. Is this because our faith leads us to feel and to behave as though this aspect were completely foreign to us and to adopt the attitude of spectators, passive, resigned and indifferent? From the earliest days of antiquity we have been accused of this—as, for example, by Cornelius Celsus, around 177–180, the earliest of the "masters of anti-Christian thought" (Origen, *C. Celsum*, VIII, 68). We can see to what lengths the Apologists of the following generation, Tertullian and others with him, went to convince their audience that the fact that a Christian considers himself a citizen of the eternal City does not necessarily lead him to desert the position he holds, by the will of God, within the human city (witness my old friend, the author of the *Letter to Diognetus*).

Even within the Christian tradition Augustinism has been accused of the same thing, as though Augustine's preoccupation with the "last things," the ultimate goals of human activity and human history, led him to neglect and despise humble temporal tasks. The accusation is as unfounded as that which stems from the fear that an emphasis on personal predestination tends to encourage spiritual lukewarmness and will lead to moral laxity. However, the fact that these fears have persisted throughout the centuries should give us pause . . . It is true that, in a certain sense, a Christian does not totally belong to the earthly city and that he cannot work in it in exactly the same way as those who envisage nothing beyond this world, but it is indispensable that we pursue this reflection further.

Let us consider things in their essence rather than concerning ourselves with the problem of locating the true danger: there will, of course, always be people who are weak and fearful and who will use the transcendental vision of Christianity as an alibi to justify their own escapism (such anemically "virtuous" people deserve the sarcasm of Nietzsche); in fact there is perhaps an historical problem in determining whether sociologically "Christian" societies have not often been used as a refuge for this type of recruit. But the tasks and the days of the earthly city are far too fascinating and absorbing— they arouse and sustain so many devouring passions ranging from love to ambition that the problem has usually been to prevent men from succumbing to it entirely. This, at any rate, has been the tendency of our spiritual tradition.

If we hope for an adequate answer to the fundamental question as we have raised it here, we shall have to lower our sights from the exalted heights of the eschatological perspective we have been talking about to the condition that is proper to man in his present situation. However fruitful the notion of inchoative eschatology may be, it is a very delicate one to handle, and it can very easily be misused. This is why we must repeatedly insist on the fact that we have not yet risen, we have not yet become completely spiritualized beings, we are still immersed in the human condition which has its own servitudes, exigencies and laws—the first of which is that we are rooted in carnal materiality—and in case we are ever tempted to forget it, our material circumstances remind us forcefully of the weight of this condition from which we cannot escape.

In this context I would like to call to mind again the invaluable experience of the monastic tradition: several collections of apothegms of the Desert Fathers have preserved the following story about Abbot Sylvanus of Sinai: a visitor was very surprised to see that the monks were busy with many different jobs and exclaimed, "Why do you work for perishable food? Did not Mary choose the better part?" The Abbot settled his visitor in a cell and gave him a book for his meditation—but nothing to eat. Meal-time came and went and the guest asked for food, whereupon Sylvanus pretended to be astonished and said, "Are you not a spiritual man who has chosen the better part? You do not need perishable food; but we who are still carnal men cannot do without something to eat, and that means that we have to work." When the guest, thoroughly embarrassed, said he was sorry, Sylvanus added, "I am glad that you recognize that Mary cannot get along without Martha and that Martha, therefore, shares the praise that is bestowed on Mary" (*Silv.* 5, P.G. 65, 40 and parallels).

Yes indeed! St. Paul had already reminded the Thessalonians of this elementary rule: ". . . not to let anyone have any food if he refused to do any work" (this verse, 2 Th 3:10, was written into the

Constitution of the Soviet Union by Stalin—memories of his semi-
nary days?). By his work, man—and the Christian is subject to this
law like everyone else—finds himself a part of a certain system of
production, an economic system, a civilization. And then again,
when we speak of food we are only speaking of the most elementary
level, the "first goods of the earth," which is an old Stoic notion that
St. Augustine developed in Book XIX of the *City of God*. But man,
if he is to be truly man, cannot be content with satisfying his most
immediate needs. He does not live by bread alone but also by other
values—esthetic and moral values—which characterize the cultural
society of which he is a part.

If this is true of a hermit, a monk, a contemplative, how much
more must it be true of an ordinary Christian, who is normally
immersed in an earthly vocation, who has a position to keep up in
society, a part to play in the world. He may suffer because of this
immersion and the demands it makes on him, which are often very
burdensome (in industrial societies work is often an overwhelming
obligation and a dehumanizing process of alienation): it is natural
that he should want to be delivered from this burden. This too is a
part of the spirituality expressed by the *Marana tha*, "Come, Lord."
On the other hand he also has to accept the fact that he must submit to these conditions, and if the temptation to escape sometimes
becomes too strong the persecutions that recur periodically bring
him back to the reality of this earthly city which demands that he
submit to it, that imposes itself on him, willy-nilly, and denies him
the right to cut himself off. Also the growing political, economic,
social and cultural awareness that is characteristic of our times makes
all this more obvious than ever. It is a fact that, by the very nature
of our human condition, we are launched into history—and now I
am taking the word history in its fullest human, earthly and
"temporal" sense. Oh, the ingenuousness of those "pure souls" who
thought they could be free of the duties of this world and avoid
"political action": we are always acting politically even when we
are most passive! In fact passivity is often the worst form of political
action.

The very notion of human nature, which includes the social

dimension we have stressed, implies that we are rooted in an historical context. Whether we are aware of it or not, we are inevitably and in a thousand different ways actors in that other history which is unfolding within the geographical and temporal dimensions of life on this earth. And the whole of our spiritual tradition imposes on us the obligation in conscience to take part in this history in full awareness and responsibility. In passing, we find ourselves coming back to the good old theology of the duty of our state, the theology of the personal vocation within which we are expected to sanctify ourselves. This is explicitly formulated in New Testament revelation: in the Gospel parables of the seed that is scattered on fertile ground, the talents that have been entrusted to each man according to his capacity and that he must put to profitable use, the authority and the work that is entrusted to each servant to be exercised during the absence of the Lord (Mk 13:34), the parable of the household and the servants to be administered by the loyal and careful steward . . .

But this is not really our problem. What we must try to make clear is the coherence of Christian thought: can we determine whether there is any connection, and, if so, can we be sure what that connection is, between the sacred history that we have defined, evoked and praised in the first part of this book and secular history (in which of course religious history still has a very considerable place) that visible history of cities, empires, nations, civilizations following on each other in empirical time? This is the true problem, and it is so obscure that Christian thought seems to be divided over the answer and has opted alternately for contradictory positions.

30. THE LIMITS OF ESCHATOLOGY

Some scholars have always been strongly tempted to give a categorically negative answer to this fundamental question: No, there is no connection between the history of civilizations and the history of salvation. They take place on totally different levels. To devote oneself to the tasks of the earthly city contributes nothing to "hastening"—the coming of the Parousia. I must say at once that I believe that this exclusive point of view is dangerously mistaken, but I can readily understand and share the concern that has led some to adopt it. It seems quite legitimate to worry, and very difficult not to do so, when one sees the supernatural meaning of history and the transcendent finality of the Church disappearing so completely from view, and when men begin to judge the Church solely in relation to its role within the earthly city and in terms of the specific finality of the latter. One can only deplore the enduring influence of the school of apologetics which started with Chateaubriand and has been consistently superficial and sometimes blasphemous. Like every other apologetic tactic, this one ended by being used to the advantage of the adversaries it was supposed to combat. Having exalted the civilizing influence of the Church within the barbarian West, one can now accuse her of being too slow to eliminate the remnants of mediaeval Christendom and to join forces with modern civilization. "The Church always seems to be behind the times in relation to the historical evolution of humanity" or, as one of my students once put it, so picturesquely: "Instead of being the locomotive, the Church is the caboose on the end of the train of history . . ."

In a more general way there has always been a pessimistic tendency within the Christian tradition, and it is the adherents of this trend who would be most likely to deny the existence of any

connection between the two ways of looking at history. Not content
with considering the tasks to which the earthly city calls or compels
us absolutely futile from the standpoint of eternal life, which they
see primarily as a prize to be won, they also see in the history of
the secular city the obsessive presence of evil, the reign of sin, the
unmistakable mark of Satan, prince of this world and this era, prince
of the time of history. Although there is a chronological coincidence
between the two, although sacred history and secular history are
taking place within the same time-dimension, nevertheless sacred
history takes place essentially or very largely in opposition to the
history of the world, in spite of and in counteraction to it. Those
who hold this view have discarded all but one of the characteristics
of the time of the Church: it remains a time of patience and persecution, a time of martyrdom. Its function is to produce and
develop, to form and temper, the saints and bring them to maturity.

Of course there is a great deal of truth—culled both from revelation and from life's experience—in this view. But we cannot allow
ourselves to be carried away and overstep the mark—like Pascal
when he went as far as to write: "O God, who allows the world and
all the things of the world to exist only for the sake of trying your
elect and punishing sinners . . ." I have to admit that this
exaggerated language might have been inspired by some of St.
Augustine's more intransigent expressions, when he endeavors to
impress upon us the limits and imperfections of all earthly goods,
even the most precious, and to save us from the mirages of im-
permanency. "And all these are but the solace of the wretched and
condemned, not the rewards of the blessed" (*City of God,* XXII,
24)— like the alcohol offered to a condemned man on the morning
of his execution!

There is, of course, a touch of rhetorical inflation here, but
prophetic inspiration sometimes has to resort to such methods when
faced with the obligation of transmitting a paradoxical message,
especially when the truth is hard to accept. It is often necessary to
remind men who are too enamored of earthly goods and false prestige
that this is all of an order totally different from that of the highest

finality of existence. To use the mathematical metaphor of Pascal: all these things tend, practically speaking, toward zero. And so historical time and cosmic space, in which the destiny of humanity is running its course, are seen simply as an occasion to do penance, to remain steadfast in fidelity, resoluteness and constancy; an occasion to exercise virtue and grow in holiness. In this view the specifically temporal work accomplished during the course of this brief pilgrimage has no value of its own whatsoever; a man's "merit" (in such a context this word becomes repulsive) is the same whether he has played ball, or scrupulously swept the convent yard during recreation; or whether, as a leader of men, he has victoriously led a great nation through a tragic period of its destiny, or, again, whether he has been an artist or a scholar who has led the human spirit to the highest peaks it can aspire to within the limits of its created nature.

In this view the cosmos and its history are nothing more than a theater, a stage-set in which the spiritual drama of humanity is being played out. The world is a sports arena, a field of manoeuvers for the army of saints. And once the spiritual saga of the saints is accomplished, the world and its time, being no longer useful, will be done away with and "the heavens are rolled up like a scroll" (Is 34:4 = Rv 6:14)—in the way one rolls up his floor mat when he has finished his gymnastics. One could quote innumerable significant passages which bear witness to such a frame of mind—from the Scriptures or the Fathers to the "eschatologists" of the last generation: history seen as an evolution toward nothingness, a river that bears men, engaged in mortal works, inexorably toward death. . . .

Even if their authors used these formulas in order to remind man that he is not on this earth simply to accomplish the works of this earth, they are not exempt from polemical excessiveness. We must beware of overstepping the limits and of concluding that whatever man accomplishes on this earth has no value either in itself or in the result obtained, but only insofar as it is useful to his spiritual advancement. I would like to borrow yet another anecdote from the literature about the Desert Fathers: John Cassian tells us of a hermit living in such a distant solitude that the baskets he wove from palm fronds, in obedience to the rule of working, accumulated until they cluttered up his cell. At the end of the year he got rid of them by burning them and then began all over again (*Inst.* X, 24). I have chosen this example because it is so obviously a very extreme case. One of the reasons why basket-weaving was the favorite occupation of the Egyptian solitaries was because this work fitted into the normal economy of Coptic society. The baskets were useful, and they had a commercial value. The money they earned was used to buy the minimum requirements in food and cloth without which the hermits, even if they lived in an orchard of date palms, could not survive. Any surplus earned by selling the baskets went to the service of the poor.

The Christian must beware of a false "angelism," which can never be anything but theoretical in any case: the daily experience of life would very soon give it the lie. We are, it is true, disciples of him who made the solemn declaration before Pilate: "Mine is not a kingdom of this world" (Jn 18:36). But a little earlier in the same Gospel, Jesus made it clear that he had no wish to withdraw his disciples from this world (17:15). Their situation, and ours, is complex as is clearly implied by the synthetic concept of inchoative eschatology that we have used to define it. In one very important sense Christians no longer belong to this world (Jn 17:14) but they remain in this world (17:11).

By the very fact of our human condition we are immersed in the world, that is in temporality, in history; in the history of a given social environment, nation or empire, in the history of a civilization. No one escapes from this, as we have seen, and anyone who claims to escape from it is deluding himself. The potentialities of our human nature only fulfill themselves in reality—the man in me only really becomes a man—when and to the extent that they take shape by using the various means for action put at their disposal by the techniques operative in the particular civilization in which they exist. Mozart would have remained a potential musician only if his Father had not set him down at a well-tuned harpsichord when he was still a child, and if he had not learned harmony and counterpoint, and if he had not known Bach and the great masters of classical music. . . .

Even if our participation in such or such a period of universal history means that we are living in the midst of a civilization ill-adapted to the demands of Christianity, or even overtly hostile to Christianity, it is not easy to break the bonds of solidarity that bind us to it. In retrospect the historian can now see the inherent contradictions, the fallacy in fact, of the position adopted by the rigorist Christians, of which Tertullian was a leading example, in the Roman Empire of the third century. At the time, they seemed so logical. All civilization of that time seemed to be contaminated by paganism, from the simplest, everyday customs (the manners in eating and drinking and dressing) to the highest institutions of society (the Emperor himself—it was unthinkable that he might one day be converted to Christianity). And it was loudly proclaimed that the Christian should have nothing to do with this world contaminated by idolatry.

That is all very well, but in the meantime Christians—and Tertullian first amongst them—lived in comfort in the peaceful Roman world of the Empire, making the most of the order imposed by a liberal administration, using all the public services that were available to them, frequenting the forum, the markets and the baths (*Apol*, 42:2). They could keep their hands clean and be content to pray for the Emperor and the salvation of the Empire; they could refuse to defile themselves by joining an army that was in the service of false gods; they could pride themselves on applying the precept: "Thou shalt not kill" to the letter because others, the pagans, enrolled in the Legions and the auxiliary forces and mounted guard at the borders to resist attack from the barbarians.

It was a radically pagan culture that was taught in the schools, and as such the Christian had no right to profess it—but Tertullian had been brought up in it, and he defended and expounded his Christian faith and his own intransigence with the arms it provided: the dialectic, the rhetoric, the mastery of verbal expression, so that, in the final analysis, he could not forbid his own Christian pupils access to the schools he denied to the teachers.

31. OUR SECULAR WORK

Because our human condition launches us into history we will necessarily be actors in history and not only spectators or onlookers (as we have seen, to refuse to act is still a type of action, often the worst type). We shall be judged according to what we have done during our brief journey on earth. Whether we be workers of the first or of the eleventh hour we have a job to do; history has put us into the vineyard of the Lord; this is our field of work. This is why, when we pray that his kingdom come, we must also pray that we may learn to "count how few days we have" and that he will "make all we do succeed" (Ps 90:12, 17).

But what is this historical work in which we are called to collaborate? Here we have to look at reality in all its stark simplicity and leave the rarefied atmosphere of abstract speculation behind. What do we mean when we speak of "working for the coming of the Kingdom," of "building the City of God"? It simply means that each one of us has to endeavor, constantly, to obey the Gospel law more perfectly. And the Gospel law is the law that has adopted the tradition handed down from the Old Testament in order to bring it to perfection, summing it up in the double injunction: to love God and to love our neighbor. As the parable of the Good Samaritan indicates, my neighbor is anyone that my generosity leads me to treat as a neighbor; in other words, every man is, by right, my neighbor. All men are my neighbors. This is the whole of our Law, and the second commandment is like the first (Mt 22:39); in fact, the second comes first in the order of action, as St. Augustine emphasizes in his commentary on the verse from St. John (I Jn

4:20): "Since a man who does not love the brother that he can see cannot love God, whom he has never seen" (*Tract. in Joh.* 17:8).

I would like my reader to believe that with this reference I am not simply giving expression to a scholarly reflex or to the homage due from a disciple. Augustinism—and this is its particular function within the Christian tradition—has its own special message in respect to this central problem, and it is important that we should hear it and bear it in mind; this unique twofold love "must be the constant object of our thoughts and of our meditation. We must cling to it; it is what we have to do and accomplish" (*Ibid*).

No area of our lives can be foreign to its influence, either in theory or in fact (except, of course, sin); we have no right to divide our lives into two parts and to keep one of them for God: "He claims the whole of you, he who gave you being" (*Serm.* 34:4 [7]). And elsewhere Augustine says, "When God commands us to love him with all our heart, all our soul and all our mind, he has not left empty of that love any part of our life, in which we could rest in the possession of another. Everything that we may be led to love must be swept away as by a torrent—the torrent of the true love of God that will not suffer being diminished by even the tiniest trickle of water turned aside from the main stream" (*De Doctr. Christ.* 1, 22 [21]).

Once we have understood this, nothing in the world of man, nothing in our own work or in the events of our life, can be thought of as neutral, indifferent or foreign to Christ's combat ("Sit at my right hand and I will make your enemies a footstool for you"). In the last analysis everything we do, everything that happens in history, belongs, in one way or another, either to the City of God or to the enemy "city." There is no third camp—at least not on the same level; for when we consider what I call the empirical data of history we look at things from a quite different point of view. They are the object not of the theologian's but of the professional historian's study: events, whether momentary or long-lasting, cities, empires, civilizations.

At this point it might be useful to remind the reader of the analysis we have already made regarding the ambivalence of time and the mystery of history: the characteristic of the "empirical data" of history is the fact that the two components are inextricably interwoven: City of God, city of evil, "these two cities are tangled together" . . . All historical action, as we have seen, can be analyzed, or rather can be broken down into, the two elements,—it being clearly understood, of course, that such an analysis or decomposition is conceivable only at the eschaton, by God himself. What we must now emphasize is the absolutely universal nature of such a principle: nothing should—and, giving all due consideration to the distressing proportion of failure that is the outcome of sin—nothing can remain extraneous to the preparation of the kingdom, the growth of the City of God. At the heart and root of every human action can be found the intention of actualizing a value which, in some way or another, partakes of the absolute values.

32. *TECHNIQUE AND THE ABSOLUTE*

I would like to take the example that can be most easily grasped, the specific sphere in which the term "history" has been most often used, that of political life. Any genuinely healthy political action must necessarily involve the attempt to promote a situation of less injustice and greater peace amongst men, in which unity gains the upper hand over divisiveness, order over arbitrariness; in which egoism gives way to the common good; in which suffering becomes less and happiness greater. . . . We are bound to recognize in such an effort to promote a little more justice—which will always, necessarily, be only human justice, imperfect and limited—a reflection of uncreated Justice, which is both a divine attribute and an absolute value.

To make myself clear I shall take as concrete an example as

possible—that of the citizens of the European countries who, during the recent colonial wars, declared themselves in favor of the independence of the oppressed peoples, and who, in doing so, flew in the face of vigorous opposition from the government and from a large portion of public opinion amongst their fellow countrymen. There were Christians amongst these people, but they were not motivated to take this stand by ingenuous and sordid considerations of self-interest—as though their witness and their action might facilitate the future evangelization of the animist or Muslim populations concerned (even supposing that this might be true, it could only be a remote and hypothetical secondary consideration). They took a stand first and foremost to promote a just cause, because the right to independence and development as a nation is the inalienable right of every nation and because the conditions under which the colonized people lived were an offense to the dignity of man. Thus, in their stand, there was an element of absolute value.

These men were not all so blind as to idealize their cause. They were ready to recognize that those who fought for freedom were not all pure, that they too committed crimes and, at the same time, that the colonial enterprise was not all bad, that it had brought some results that were intrinsically good. Shame on anyone who uses the principle of ambivalence that we have studied to justify his refusal to take a stand (in this instance it would have amounted to taking the side of colonialism against independence)!

I am ready to venture that the starting point of any political and, more generally, any historical action (the positive aspect that is, the affirmation and development of values come later) is the literally *unbearable, intolerable* nature of evil. It is a pressing duty that admits of no indifference or slackness, to do whatever we can to lessen suffering, injustice and sin whenever we see a way to do so.

If we meet a wounded man by the side of the road, it is not permissible to go on our way. For once the Gospel and the laws of men are in agreement on this point. Starting from this instance which happens every day (there are not so many brigands on the highways as in the days of the Good Samaritan, but there are more accidents) one can generalize and apply the same principle to the more complex problems of war and peace amongst nations, social justice, etc.

The fullness of love that should inspire all our acts must be a real and concrete love, not just a question of wishful thinking or theory, and it must express itself in deeds. Whatever we may think of certain formulations which seem to contradict this in the writings of the spiritual masters, an ethic of intention is not a truly Christian ethic. St. James' severe admonition makes this very clear: "if one of the brothers or one of the sisters is in need of clothes and has not enough food to live on, and one of you says to them, 'I wish you well; keep yourself warm and eat plenty,' without giving them these bare necessities of life, then what good is that?" (2:15–16.)

A very common type of Christian spirituality, as it has been popularized (and somewhat degraded in the process) has all too often ignored this fundamental exigency and neglected everything that is temporally and historically efficacious. The danger, in this type of spirituality, is that one can too readily believe that one has reached his goal and fail to give due regard to the eschatological mystery and the servitudes stemming from its delayed fulfillment. In other words, it leads too easily to the feeling that one has the right to substitute God's point of view for the point of view of man, who is still a pilgrim. A human act (and this holds good for every act that takes place in history, beginning with the most ordinary acts of daily life) cannot be "credited" to the account of the City of God simply because it was dedicated to this supreme finality by a general good intention—a "blanket" offering, a "My God I offer you this day . . ." at the beginning and end of the day or even at the beginning and end of the specific action. This hasty spiritualization "applied" to the outside of an action fails to impregnate the action itself at any depth and often never goes beyond the stage of being a pious wish or pure verbalism.

Just as, earlier, we referred to the human condition and the laws which govern it, we must now respect the nature of things. A concern for efficacity means that we must move into the sphere of technique: in imitation of, and moved by, the love that God has shown for me, I want to exercise my love in favor of my neighbor, my brother. This love will either be forever a potentiality without practical effect or, to become act, it will have to take concrete form and be exerted within the framework of one of the techniques that I am in a position to master according to the particular environment and civilization in which I live. I do not want to overload this meditation with too many erudite details; however, I think that it is useful to mention in passing that this notion of "technique," taken in a very broad sense (it does not apply only to industry but also to science, art and thought), is a legacy from the classical tradition: it is a translation of the Greek *teknai* and the Latin *artes*.

It is perhaps in precisely this domain that sociologically Christian societies have to make their greatest effort to correct their attitudes and that they can learn most from the secular society around them. The traditional, sociologically Christian milieus have not yet sufficiently recognized and respected the existence of an ontological level proper to the domain of technique. How many religious superiors have been ready to accept the idea that obedience made up for a lack of competence in their subordinates? But if we are not going to content ourselves with sprinkling some pious intentions over our work—if, on the contrary, we want the value, in terms of the City of God, to enter into the heart of the action itself—efforts at spiritualizing it must begin by respecting the autonomy of a technique which has its own laws, its own internal logic as well as its own inertia and resistance, before trying to bend it to the service of our own purposes.

At this juncture we come back to the social, collective aspect of the human condition: even our most personal work, if it is really and honestly carried out with a view to efficacity, cannot be separated from the structures of the surrounding civilization. This civilization offers us the possibility of working within a certain number of techniques that have reached a certain stage of development after a long and often complex evolution. It is up to us to take the tools that are available and put them to the best possible use, order-

ing them to the higher ends to which we have consecrated our own
life. Thus in the field of medicine: Ben Sira emphasized that although healing comes from God, the doctor has also been created
by God (Si 38:1–8). A healthy theology cannot give approval to
sects such as the Jehovah's Witnesses who claim to trust in God and
refuse to use the technical skills that God has given to men.

If this is self-evident for psychosomatic medicine, it is no less true
in regard to "social" medicine. To the extent to which the human
sciences—political economy, for example—provide us with means for
working on the social body that were unknown to earlier generations—just as they were unaware of asepsis and antibiotics—it is up
to us to use our ingenuity in applying them to heal the ills that have
always plagued the social body. We should not, as has too often
been done, consider the social sciences and Christian charity to be
mutually exclusive (even taking the word charity, translation of the
New Testament *agape*, in the vulgar, debased sense that it now has).
There will always, alas! be plenty of opportunity to exercise charity:
"The poor will always be with you," not to mention the sub-
proletariat on which the prosperity of the developed nations rests and
whose existence makes possible the relative liberation of an elite
amongst the working people. And can we not foresee the day when
psychiatric clinics will take the place of prisons and deportation
camps! Whatever system may be devised for the management
and exploitation of the secular city, there will always be a marginal
percentage of those who cannot adapt to society, who will fail and
are poor. Generous hearts will always be able to help them. But it
would be just as erroneous to neglect the techniques of insurance
and social security that are now available to us as it would be to rely
only on prayer for the cure of diseases for which we now have
serums and vaccination.

As mentioned above, these techniques are products of a complex
evolution in which more than one causal sequence has been operative, some inherent to the technique itself, others being expressions
of the various influences superimposed by the civilization within
which each technique has been developed. This explains why they
now impose themselves on us with an inevitability that is akin to

that of physical nature. It is not that we are totally unable to modify and influence their further development, especially over a long period, but that this influence will only show its effects very slowly. In the long run even the most violent and far-reaching revolutions have had to take this inertia into account. Think of the delirious excesses of proletarian culture in the early years of the Soviet regime: experience was to show that it is not easy to create an entirely new form of culture and a new educational system. By February 1921 Lenin was already recommending that Russian youth return to a study of the classics, Pushkin and Nekrassov. And so the present stage of development of the different techniques imposes a certain framework, which is often very rigid, and thereby limits the effectiveness of our efforts. To take only two examples: it was not at all easy in the days when liberal capitalism was at its height, to be a "Christian employer." It was not enough just to hang a crucifix on the walls of the factory, to facilitate the reception of the sacraments or to organize and finance charitable works. The employer was part of an economic system (the factory had to make a profit and survive competition), and he was forced to exploit his workers and be a source of injustice and further poverty. Although he may have wished with all his heart to work for the coming of the kingdom, in actual fact he contributed to the ravages of evil in the world. This had been the fate of the first Christian Emperors: the fact that the Imperial standards were surmounted by the monogram of Christ in a crown of laurels did nothing to obviate another fact, that the Imperial State was a somber totalitarian machine and the instrument of police and fiscal terrorism.

In both cases it was the system itself that should have been changed: it should have been possible to work effectively to transform it, even if this could only have been accomplished little by little, almost imperceptibly. But in both cases "social" medicine was not yet sufficiently developed. The situation was analogous to that in which medical science found itself with regard to small-pox before Jenner, or with regard to diphtheria before the work of Roux and Ramon.

This leads us to a new and deeper, more vital understanding of the traditional moral precept concerning the "duty of our state" that we mentioned earlier. If we wish to hasten the coming of the Day of the Lord it is not enough for us to offer our work to God, even if we accomplish it with perfect professional conscience. It must have value in itself and of itself. It must contribute effectively to diminishing the power of evil, suffering, injustice and sin in human society and to developing the positive counterparts of a greater well-being, a higher level of being, that will truly be a hymn to the glory of God. And this depends, in the first place, on our technical skill and our compliance with the laws that govern this particular field, this specific level of "art."

It also demands intelligence, initiative, a capacity for invention and creation. It is up to us to be attentive to the "signs of the times" (John XXIII has solemnly reminded us of this phrase of St. Matthew, 16:3). It is up to us to exploit the present moment to the hilt. If you remember, this was the meaning that we found in Paul's injunction (Ep 5:16 and Col 4:5). It is up to us to make the most of the openings available to us in the spontaneous evolution of techniques. Of course, as we have seen, this is not always easy, "for the times are evil" and history has not always placed us in very comfortable circumstances. All the more reason to be watchful and to seize every opportunity that offers itself. And this is valid in all areas of human activity: once again, in the final analysis, there is nothing in human activity, there is no aspect of history, that will not one day come under the scrutiny of the eschatological judgment and be broken down until it is seen for what it was: a contribution or a hindrance to the development of the City of God. Nothing can escape this scrutiny: in the last analysis it is because nothing in history is purely "secular." Everything can be either sanctified or profaned.

The value judgment that will be passed on our action in history will have to consider that action within the framework of its concrete reality, in its living context in the complex web of structures superimposed on each other—from the personal life through the different levels of collective life all the way to the level of that vast phenomenon that can be called civilization. Our theology of history cannot be detained by the classical distinctions of theologians, between nature and supernature, the temporal and the spiritual, the sacred and the profane—or, to be more precise, between what belongs immediately to the sphere of God's kingdom and what concerns only the purely secular values of mankind that can be isolated and examined in themselves and considered as constituting intermediary goals, subordinated to the supreme goal of man's supernatural destiny. It is not that I mean to dispute such a distinction; it has its own value in truth and it is useful in other areas. But there is a difference between the analysis of the ontological structure of being and the historical judgment that can be made of human action, envisaged in its totality and not in its component parts.

It seems to me that in this particular area Augustinism has its own message and a significant place in the Christian spirituality of our times. St. Augustine's tendency to see man's supreme end as his only end has often been remarked. He tends to slide rapidly over the intermediate stages in the path that leads a man to his God, a sinner to salvation. An Augustinian will always have some misgivings when he sees philosophers lingering over a definition of this intermediate level, the strictly human level of temporal action. He will always fear that one might spend too much time and find too much satisfaction on this level and forget the urgent necessity of raising oneself to the higher level. After all, this is the downhill path that man's weakness inclines him to follow. Especially today: this is a constant temptation in this dechristianized world, in this civilization so passionately enamored of the power of earthly things, so obsessed with their problems and single-mindedly absorbed in their exigencies.

It has never been profitable to imagine that one could isolate, except by abstraction, any area that is purely the domain of human nature—in which man is free to fulfill his vocation as man and which would provide a common ground in which Christians could work together with all men of good will in a common enterprise. It is true, a Christian cannot easily feel completely at home in the world. We shall never make very good allies for the others: in every enterprise we undertake with others we are quick to recognize the point at which our common project has gone awry, when the means used compromise the ends we are pursuing, when violence, the will to power, evil in a word, gains the upper hand and forces us to withdraw.

Augustinian thought vigorously opposes the tendency to forget the historical, concrete situation which is the lot of fallen man awaiting Redemption. The historian, unfortunately, has to acknowledge that he is right. Let us take the instance that can most easily be observed, that of the relations between the Church as a visible society and the secular State: the periods in history during which the two have lived in unison have been very brief—I mean in which they have lived in a truly harmonious equilibrium, not just in outward tranquility—whereas governments and kings calling themselves "Christian" have been legion. Under Constantine, for instance: at the end of the Council of Nicaea all the problems seemed to have been resolved and then, three or four years later, Arius and his followers were restored to grace and Orthodoxy had become suspect and subject to persecution. . . .

To speak in a more speculative vein, we might ask what human nature, what man, we are talking about. Empirically, historically speaking, we only know human nature wounded by sin, which grace seeks to heal and raise to a higher level. We cannot see man in a stable situation, in a state that can be defined and located once and for all. We can only see him as he is in the midst of the battle, in the course of his life-drama, divided within himself, torn between damnation and salvation. This is an elementary datum which we must not forget at the peril of forgetting that all temporal activities, even those whose immediate object concerns only problems which are proper to this life on earth exist only in a human subject and that this child of Adam in whom they exist is one and the same who is called to become a child of God. No activity of a technical order can exist in isolation. They are all part of a man's life and partake of his destiny. And his destiny lies beyond the horizons of this earth.

33. A HIERARCHY OF TECHNIQUES

This principle, like every deep truth, should be handled with a certain care; otherwise it may be replaced by a caricature. Even if it is true that everything can and must be used for the service of the Kingdom to come (and which is, by the same token, already amongst us), it would be ingenuous and crude to consider all techniques to be on the same plane. There is a hierarchy amongst the different techniques which stems from their very nature and according to whether they are susceptible to being oriented more or less directly toward spiritual ends and impregnated with spiritual values. If I were asked to give an indication of such a classification, I would suggest that we distinguish four broad categories: I shall indicate very briefly the ambivalence which characterizes each one and show how each can be turned from its true end and join forces with the Enemy:

1. On the highest level I would place contemplation, prayer and all the manifestations of the religious life properly so called. On this level the danger is one that has been so clearly recognized and denounced, this time quite rightly, by the critics of "false" religion, by which virtue becomes Pharisaism, prayer becomes the unleashing of egoism, and religious practices become pure routine or magic gestures. If one disregards its exaggerations and polemical high-spirits, Dr. Robinson's *Honest to God* is a very good translation of the Pauline verse in Galatians, 6:7: "Don't delude yourself into thinking God can be cheated."

2. Immediately below this first level I would place the techniques that are most directly capable of helping man to rise to the highest levels of his own nature and of orienting him toward the first level of activity: on the one hand, speculative thought, philosophy, science (as knowledge of the structure and possibilities of the created

131

cosmos and not as a means of action on it); on the other hand, art
and the esthetic experience. In either area the temptation is very
great to turn these techniques away from their spiritual fulfillment
and, blasphemously, to transform them into idols.

3. Next come the techniques that can be classed as belonging to
the political, social and economic spheres (in which one can include
hygiene and medicine) and which are specifically engaged in the
organization of human life insofar as it is temporal, endeavoring
to make it as good as it can be within the limits of the temporal
condition. It is not necessary to refer at length to the *City of God*
and its bitter attack on the will to power: the possible perversions
are all too obvious and widely documented by historical experience.
There is no aspect of these techniques that cannot be turned to the
service of evil. The ancients had neither heroin nor L.S.D., but
they already knew that pharmacology could produce as many
harmful drugs as remedies (*City of God* XXII, 24:3).

4. Finally, on the lower end of the scale, I would place the techniques which, at first sight, appear to be the most material, such as
agriculture and industry; in fact, almost everything which modern
man thinks of when he uses the word "technique," and which, from
our point of view, can only be fully justified to the extent to which
they are effectively used for the service of man, in order to enable
him to engage in the use of the higher techniques. Much could be
said about this and the theology of history will surely be severely
critical of our industrial civilization in which techniques end by
becoming autonomous finalities and man is shackled to their service,
the master having become the slave, subject to the machines that
were invented to free him.

This is, quite obviously, only a first and summary sketch. If we
were to pursue this analysis, we would have to draw a distinction
between the various applications of any given technique, for a technique can be classed on different levels of the hierarchical scale
according to the different uses that are made of it. Take the case of
cooking, for instance: if it is defined simply as the art of preparing
food, it will have to be classed in the lowest rank, in relation to

the "basic natural good" of physical health. We might emphasize that even on this level it can well be the object of a value judgment: it is not enough that the pangs of hunger be assuaged; food must also serve to provide a balanced diet. Certain civilizations have been unable to attain even this objective: in many parts of Africa children lack proteins when they are weaned, and in many Asian countries the polished rice deprives people of essential B1 vitamins and makes them prone to beriberi.

But amongst highly civilized peoples this same technique can reach the level of an art—it is the case in China and in France. On this level ambivalence rears its head all over again: evil gains the upper hand if this art is used for the sake of concupiscence or vanity—gastronomy then becomes the systematic cultivation of one of the seven or eight capital sins. But it can also become one of the refinements by which man shows himself to be civilized and by which he raises the purely biological, animal function of nourishment to the esthetical level and the level of human relations.

However, even if we refine this notion of a hierarchy of techniques to the highest possible degree, it still cannot provide sufficient evidence to make a final judgment. The contribution that any historical act may make to the accomplishment of time cannot be evaluated simply in relation to the technique used and the position it occupies on the above scale. When music, for instance, becomes sacred music—which, in theory, means that it moves up from the second category to the first—it is not in any way obvious that it thereby becomes more closely dedicated to the service of God. Take the classical example of the duet "*La ci darem la mano*" in Mozart's *Don Giovanni*: technically this is a scene from a comic opera and, to quote from the script, a commonplace of lewd morals of a very ordinary variety—in other words, it is a seduction scene. And yet an enthusiast taking this page of Mozart for solitary meditation at the keyboard might well find that it affords him an authentic spiritual experience. For him it could be a model of the highest form of music, which is essentially religious. On the other hand, the public recital of such or such a baroque magnificat, even in a liturgical context, if it is too splendidly orchestrated and too brilliantly executed, can bring us back to the level of profane, or profaned, music.

34. THE NOTION OF USUS

The role, the significance and the value of an historical action depend not only on its technical qualities, considered in themselves, but also on the complex conditions within which it is carried out in history. A glass of water is, if you wish, in itself one of those elementary goods that are ordered to the well-being of human nature. But it becomes a very different value according to whether it is drunk, on an Autumn day in the verdant English countryside or on a day of crushing summer heat in the middle of the Sahara. When the good Samaritan gives it to a wounded man, dying of thirst, it becomes charged with a very high value. In quite another context (I am thinking, for example, of the ascetics of the Egyptian desert), it can become the object of ungovernable concupiscence. It all depends on the use—the *usus*—that is made of it.

We should delve a little deeper into this very fruitful notion introduced by the teaching of St. Augustine at this point; *usus* is not only understood as the good (or bad) use of things in the sense in which a vague kind of moralism might speak of it. It is the full implementation, in a synthesis of concrete circumstances, which transforms the technical operation into a fact of civilization.

"Building houses"—this is one of the examples St. Thomas chose to show that man, in his wounded nature, can accomplish a certain, particular good "by virtue of his nature" (I^a II^{ae} qu 109, art. 2)— is never, per se, an historical action. It is simply an integral element of a larger project which contains other values directly pertinent to the kingdom. A house built by a group of friends who pool their labor in a common endeavor to provide a decent lodging for their families, is quite a different matter from one built by a contractor motivated by capitalistic speculation, inhumanly exploiting a helpless sub-proletarian population for his own profit—which happened, for example, in France in the 60's with the migrant workers from Algeria and Portugal who had no work permits.

But let us take a rather more complex case—a scientific discovery, the theory of atomic fission, for instance: ontologically speaking this is something good in itself insofar as it is part of knowledge and is charged with a value of truth. But it has no existence in reality, historically speaking, separated from the minds of the scientists who have conceived it, who think of it and possess it, and from the cultural milieu which receives it and will proceed to use it for certain given ends. This example demonstrates the notion of *usus* on several levels; will atomic energy be used to take the place of coal and oil for peaceful purposes, or will it be used in the service of blind destruction, death and a rampant will to power? But even before the discovery has gone beyond the laboratory walls, in some members of the scientific team it will induce a demonic elation giving rise to blasphemy, whereas for a Christian it will be an occasion of—better, it will transform itself into—a hymn of adoration and praise. The discovery of sinanthropus when exploited by Teilhard de Chardin spontaneously tends toward the Omega point and sings the glory of the Creator. In the heyday of scientism it would have served to foster an atheistic interpretation by Darwin and would have become an argument against the historical value of the first chapters of Genesis.

We must be careful that a concern for clarity and precision in the ontological analysis of techniques does not lead us to forget that they are all human activities. They have been created by the genius and skill of men for the purpose of resolving the problems of this life as it unfolds in space and in time. Activities of a technical order are part of human actions, purposes and realizations. They are part of men's destiny and men's lives. We can only measure how positive and valuable a contribution to the promotion and progress of history is made by such or such an event, if we look at it from this concrete point of view.

However it is not for us to encroach upon the judgment of eschatology. It is quite enough that we know and understand that in the most pedestrian, and apparently most profane, things of our daily lives we can and must work at an undertaking whose fruits, stored in eternal dwelling places, will never rot. The beautiful formula that St. Augustine once used in a sermon, can be applied to all historical action: "The architect builds a dwelling destined to endure, by means of provisional scaffolding" (*Serm.* 362, 7). Augustine himself applies this to the special historical events which go to make up the central panel of the triptych, those which marked the Incarnation and Passion of Our Lord Jesus Christ. They are events that took place in time and they belong, now, to the past, but their efficacious properties endure eternally. But is this not equally true of the whole of the history of salvation, and especially of our own share in its promotion? Everything that we accomplish within time is destined to fade away, just as the figure of this world will fade away. But what is recorded in terms of the City of God, the part of absolute value which, with the grace of God, we have been able to put into our work and develop through it—even if, unfortunately, it has been diminished or compromised by sin—this will not crumble away. It will appear intact on the Day of Judgment.

However, we should, perhaps, eliminate a rather artificial and unnecessarily disparaging note in the image of the "provisional scaffolding." Certainly we must retain the distinction of the different orders: compared to the eschatological triumph, of course, earthly victories, the great events of history, seem very ordinary—*modica videntur,* is the expression used by St. Thomas Aquinas when, toward the end of his career, he pronounced judgment on the value of his own theology. (At least, this is the version given by the most reliable sources.[26] Legend has elaborated on the story and

---

[26] *Vitae,* G. de Tocco (47, p. 120 Prümmer), B. Gui (27, p. 193), P. Calo (24, p. 43). It was in the Process of canonization (79, p. 377, Laurent) that the word *Modica* is replaced by *paleae*—but this is only a third-hand account.

has him say: "It is all straw"—which is exaggerated and therefore false. *Modica:* a reality that is unpretentious, but, in its own order, positive and real and not just a by-product, as straw is in comparison to the grain.) Temporal history loses nothing of its reality or inherent dignity with the recognition of this truth. After all, the history of salvation has only one subject—man himself—and its object is the glory of God or, to be more precise, God's glory in and by men and, through the mediation of man, by the cosmos. Human history, seen from our position on earth, is simply the history of man, who has to be saved. I would go so far as to say that it is the material cause of sacred history—the marble which must be hewn and polished into a statue.

35. THE CARNAL CITY AND THE CITY OF GOD

We are still left with one persistent problem: we have great difficulty in saying anything very precise about the exact relationship between matter and form or, to be more accurate, between the temporal unfolding of history on earth and the growth of the City of God, which we cannot see but which, by faith, we confess as being very real. The fact that this is a difficulty is attested to by the multiplicity of formulas that have been proposed to express this relationship. The very fact that they are so numerous shows that contemporary Christian thought is still groping for a solution to this problem, which is essential from so many points of view.

Thus, J. V. Langmead Casserley: "Secular history (and by secular history must be understood all of terrestrial history with its religious as well as its specifically temporal components) is the means by which, with which and through which sacred history moves ever nearer to its end."[27] Is it then simply a means subordinate to its

[27] J. V. Langmead Casserley, op. cit., p. 65.

end? In a sense this is perfectly true: "sacred" history is not accomplished independently of everyday history as though it were outside and apart from it. But to speak of secular history as simply the instrumental cause of sacred history is a view that is too extrinsic. It is the very substance of man's secular history that must be saved. Some part of it, in our eyes the essential part of it, will enter the kingdom. It is not just an instrument or a tool that can be abandoned once the work it has been used for is accomplished.

The exaggerated terms used by Karl Barth in 1926 in the youthful fervor of his reaction against liberal theology were even more equivocal: he vigorously defended the idea that history was only a game which man, because of his terrestrial condition, was obliged to play, but which is the pursuit of an impossible goal (heaven on earth, we may add). It is a game, he said, "a serious game but a game nevertheless, that is to say a symbolic activity which, in the final analysis, has no real end and whose value derives, not from the end to be aimed at but from that which the activity symbolizes and signifies."[28] This is a hasty and somewhat contemptuous judgment of the specifically human finality of historical activity. But behind this judgment one can sense the near-obsession with transcendency that so strongly marked Barth's work: the greatest concession he could make at the time was to refrain from relegating the whole of history into the category of sin. But in the very excessiveness of his expression he was reaching out for something true: in its own way this formulation expresses the ideas we were attempting to make clear earlier when we said that the ultimate value of our actions lies in what can be recorded in terms of the City of God. In spite of the ineradicable presence of sin, in spite of all our inadequacies and failures, the element of the absolute which we emphasized really and truly dwells within them. Man's work on earth is more than just a sign, it bears within itself values which flow out beyond the bounds of time and which, even now, have reached the dwelling assigned to them in the Father's house.

[28] Karl Barth, *Theology and the Church; Shorter Writings*, N.Y., Harper & Row, 1962.

But Karl Barth would not have gone to such lengths at the end of his life—as a thinker grows older he becomes wiser! Readers of his work have noticed that his judgment of history became more and more positive, especially in his later works. I remember talking to him about Mozart, several years ago, and he used the word "parable" (one cannot say that this music is wholly enclosed in sin but it is not yet, properly speaking, the kingdom—only a parable of the kingdom). Yves Congar also dwells on this same word, as I suppose, quite independently. Speaking of successful enterprises of the human city, he wonders whether they can be "anything but a kind of parable of the kingdom and its justice and whether the Gospel can be translated in terms of an adequate program of secular enterprises."[29] The parables certainly express the truth of the Kingdom of God, but in a veiled form, and the truth is only unveiled by transposition. This image from the Gospel is wholly admirable, but perhaps it does not do justice to what is really already established in the time of the Church, in this period of inchoative eschatology. It is not only a figure of speech it is a concrete reality that a percentage—however minimal it may be and however impossible it may be for us to determine the sum—of authentic justice, an echo and a reflection of Justice itself, is present in specific political and social actions.

And then there is this other image which Etienne Gilson suggests as a conclusion and which is perhaps even more expressive: "The City of men can only arise in the shadow of the Cross, as a suburb of the City of God."[30] The suburb is not the mediaeval city lying within the security of its fortifications, but it is very close to it.

We have access to the walled city by going through the suburb, it surrounds the city as a husk surrounds the kernel.

But it is the poet Péguy who puts it most perfectly. His hesitations and his groping repetitions lead us along the path he

[29] Congar, *Laypeople in the Church; a Study for the Theology of the Laity,* Westminster, Md., Newman Press, 1957.
[30] E. Gilson, *Les metamorphoses de la Cité de Dieu,* Louvain, 1952, p. 291.

took in his own exploration of the mystery. Let me quote the
famous lines from *Eve*, at the opening of the *Prayer for Us
Carnal Men* which his death endowed, retrospectively, with an
aura of prophecy:

> Happy the men who died in the great battles,
> Stretched out on the ground before God.
> Happy the men who died on a last high place,
> Amidst all the trappings of a solemn burial.
>
> Happy the men who died for their carnal cities,
> For they are the body of the city of God . . .

"The body"? Yes, in a way. If the Christians, by which we mean
the saints, are the soul of the world, of the carnal city, as the
Letter to Diognetus has it, then the city can be said to be their
body. However, I feel that the imagery is too bold, for we are
not speaking of a body which has received the promise of the
resurrection—we have absolutely no guarantee that the temporal
structures which have served to bring holiness to fulfillment will
be found, as structures, transfigured in eschatology in the way
that human personality will be, both in body and in soul. But
the poet seems to have felt this for he takes up the thought again
and corrects it:

> Happy the men who died for their hearth
>   and their fire,
> And the poor honors of their fathers' houses.
> For they are the image and the beginning
> And the body and the essay of God's house.

Whatever Péguy himself may have meant by this (in the exacer-
bated nationalism that was rife in Europe in 1913–1914 he could
hardly avoid attaching exaggerated ontological value to the earthly
homeland) his groping phrases end by circling the reality fairly
well: image of the City of God? Yes, our earthly cities do strive to
become this to the extent to which they see themselves as an ideal

that gives flesh, through men and things, to values which partake of the eternal values. The City of God will not suddenly appear, created in a flash by the will of God. On the contrary, God wishes this city to be constructed slowly, layer by layer, stone by (living) stone, throughout the duration of human history. As we have seen already, this is the meaning and the significance of human history. Honor to the poet, then, whose intuition was so rich, even if a little lacking in precision, and who grasped the essential. He even suggested the radical imperfection and, as we shall see, the inevitable failure of such an attempt when he writes, at the end: ". . . and the essay of God's house."

36. ACTION AND ITS AMBIGUITY

For my part I shall not attempt to compete with Péguy. But even without hoping to achieve a more brilliant formulation, let us attempt, nevertheless, to pursue this analysis a little further. At the beginning we built our argument on a consideration of the human condition. Man is not on earth simply to build empires and elaborate civilizations, although the reason for his being on earth finds its accomplishment while he is engaged in those activities. We can observe the human condition only from within societies which have all, always, been faced with the task of developing the planet, of establishing order amongst the men who inhabit it, and for this end have had to use certain techniques whose stage of development has been used by the ethnologist or the historian to define the type of life characteristic of any given society. But since man is also, by nature, a creature who has a capacity for God, the work of civilization contains a component that partakes of the absolute, which is present, as we have seen, in all action, even the most specifically temporal. Every civilization seeks to realize certain values which go to make up its greatness and, from the theological point of view we have adopted, its eschatological justification.

But having reminded ourselves of all this, we then perceive that the problem of action is resolved as soon as it is stated—on the theoretical level only, of course. Difficulties arise and multiply as soon as we move from theory to practice—and the solution is that each of us must work, to the best of his ability, in the technical field in which he is competent, to serve the love of God and the love of other men, his brothers. And he must do this precisely within this earthly city, within the historical situation in which he finds himself. To the extent to which we believe in the all-powerful goodness of God we realize that it is not by chance that we have made our appearance in a given moment of history and that we are, thereby, faced with certain problems. God has willed this in a special way for each one of us. And the specificity of our insertion in history defines the task that has been entrusted to us and that is so noble and so vast that we have no right to abandon it (*Letter to Diognetus* 6:10).

For the sake of anyone who may be surprised that I insist so much on this point, which may well seem self-evident, I would like to recall to what extent the conservative, or rather reactionary, thinking which prevailed in the majority of our traditionally Christian milieus went astray when it had to face up to the emergence of the modern world. The predominant reaction was to deplore the "evils of the day." The Christian view of history, which is essentially forward-looking, had paradoxically become dimmed. Christians no longer lived in the impatient and joyous expectation of the parousia. Instead they looked back to the past and clung with nostalgic devotion to any traces or remnants of the past that had managed to survive. They were consumed with regret for restorations that had failed: Oh, if only we could have lived before 1789 and the abominable Revolution! Better still, before 1715!:

> *Oh, Wisdom of a Louis Racine, how I envy you!*

(Poor Lélian! his *Wisdom* is an excellent example of the average orthodox mentality in the years 1874–1881).

Not to have been born in the decline of the great Century . . .
No. That Century was gallican and Jansenist!
It is to the Middle Ages, vast and sensitive . . .

But what am I saying? We should have lived in the good old days of My Lord, Saint Louis. . . . As though there were ever a time in which it has been easy to be really Christian, as though a time could exist in history in which man would not have to struggle through "evil days" (Ep 5:16).

No, it is here and now that the Lord has willed that we be and it is in the specific historical—sociological, cultural and technical—context in which he has placed us that we have the task to work in his Vineyard and to show ourselves loyal and watchful servants of the task that he, the Master of the house, has entrusted to us (Mt 24:45). And now let us stop using parables and speak in direct language: if it is written: "Set your hearts on his kingdom first, and on his righteousness" (Mt 6:33)—the fundamental law of the Christian life—we must also realize that this precept is addressed to men and that it is within the human condition that it must be obeyed. Like everyone else the Christian must exercise his human calling and shoulder the responsibilities and duties imposed on him by his country, his social milieu, his family and his profession. It is within this network of relations and nowhere else that he can effectively serve, and in the first place meet, his fellows—and the Lord.

It is perfectly true that his specifically spiritual function in history—the sacerdotal role we have already discussed—must overflow the immediate, specifically temporal finality of his work. But this role can be assumed fully only from within. If the cup is to overflow, it must first of all be filled to the brim . . . We have now reached the heart of the matter, and it is very important that we should understand each other, so I would like to forestall a possible equivocation: the figure I have just used and which, like every comparison, is less than perfect, must not be taken too extrinsically, as though the kingdom were joined to the human level of life like something quite extraneous that could be added or taken away at will. That is certainly true on the ontological level (the level of nature is separate and distinct from the level of super-nature), but that is not how it is known and lived historically, existentially. The encounter with the kingdom and its exigencies takes place not on the outside of specifically human action but within its very heart.

For whatever may be the field in which this action is exerted— political life, scientific research, esthetic experience—everyday life with its monotonous, uncomplicated work, as we have seen, necessarily brings into play values which contain elements of the absolute —justice, truth, love. In this way the things of this earth partake, in a partial but very real way, of that which will be inaugurated definitively and for all eternity at the eschaton.

In order to stay within the bounds of this analysis, we must remember what we have already learned concerning the radical ambivalence of the empirical data of history. We do not have the power, at this time, to distinguish the threads of the City of God which are woven into the fabric of human history as we know and live it. Only the eschatological Judge has the power to discern the intertwining threads of the two cities . . . As they appear within the observable field of history, the two cities remain inextricably tangled together, which in the practical order leads to many distressing difficulties.

It is no easy matter to dedicate oneself solely to the service of the City of God. The kernel of absolute value lying at the heart of every human enterprise is so deeply buried in a mass of contingencies which condition and restrict it and which threaten to compromise it. But this is not the worst: even the highest human virtues can be reduced to vicious caricatures of themselves when they enter into partnership with the forces of evil. Thus, for instance, the feudal dedication of self, loyalty to a leader, devotion, renunciation to the point of self-sacrifice . . . if the leader is motivated by a demonic will to power (as in Germany, thirty years ago, when the leader's name was Hitler).

And so, once again, we come up against the problem of civilization. If, as we have said, even the most personal human action is necessarily channeled through the mold of a given technique, it is conditioned by the stage of development of this technique and, in a more general way, by the overall context of the prevailing civilization. The situation in which a Christian finds himself can become extremely ambiguous. We have already mentioned the case of the Christian industrial employer who was a prisoner of the capitalistic system and that of an Emperor in the fourth century, and we could have quoted many other examples. Technique and Christianity can reach the point of being totally in contradiction. There are, at any rate, some quite obvious incompatibilities, and during the early centuries of our era the Church listed the trades or professions which were an impediment to baptism.

If we reread these canonical texts, however—Chapter 16 of the *Apostolic Tradition* by Hippolytus of Rome, for example—we can immediately see the tremendous complexity of the problem: "brothel-keeper"? Of course, that is obvious. "The painter and the sculptor, if they persist in making idols" (what artist is not tempted at times?). "The actor . . ." (we would be far more indulgent, at least in theory, today. But what about the star who becomes an idol?). "School teachers": we have already seen this case with regard to Tertullian. At that time the whole culture was pagan, and yet the Christians recognized even then that they could not do without it. "The soldier who is in danger of spilling blood, the magistrate who has the power to condemn a man to death". . . We can see that the question is not so simple.

The degree of incompatibility is obviously variable according to the overall climate of a given civilization whose dominant trends can influence any technique to the point of hindering and correcting or, inversely, promoting such or such an aspect. This can change the value and, therefore, the role in "history"—in the fullest sense of the word—of any given technique, and determine the negative or positive contribution it can make to the development of the City of God.

And so a Christian has no right to be indifferent to the work that has to be done on this level, since the criticism and transformation of the city condition the efficacy of his action to a very large extent. And this is especially true if one looks at the fate generally reserved for the common run of men. The exceptional being, the hero or the saint, will always triumph, over even the most entangled situations, by a creative decision. But what about the great mass of our fellow men, the poor and the uneducated? It is these especially who are, in advance, victims or beneficiaries of historical conditioning.

37. CHRISTIAN CIVILIZATION

All this now leads us to consider a question that is particularly difficult but that we cannot avoid. It is no longer the question of civilization in general but that of Christian civilization or, to state it more precisely, of Christian influence in the matter of civilization. Whenever the number of Christians in any given society begins to reach sociologically appreciable proportions, whenever they become more than a small, suspect minority and move out of the ghettos created by their own refusal of the pagan environment as well as by society's distrust, then the Christian ideal begins to react upon the phenomenon of "civilization." When we speak of "Christians" in this context we cannot, with equal truth, use the term "the saints." We are now talking of those who profess the Christian faith, who are Christian in name—and our own experience as sinners and lukewarm Christians has taught us how much ambiguity there is in our theoretical profession of faith because of our own ambivalence. As soon, then, as the Christians become a minority strong enough to spread its activities beyond the strictly apostolic and cultural sphere—and all the more so when they make up the vast majority of the population (there seems to be no instance in history in which they have ever been one hundred percent of the population; even in the midst of mediaeval Christen-

dom there was the stubborn presence of Jewish communities)—
then the Christian ideal attempts to impose certain patterns on
techniques, institutions and mores in conformity with evangelical
norms. This, at least, is what they intend and wish, it is what they
hope and believe they are doing. This takes place unconsciously
at first, becoming gradually and progressively systematic. An effort
is made to act upon the civilization and transform it in reality and
in depth, to make it the beginning, the image, the incarnation of
the City of God . . .

In every instance in history in which we come across a milieu
of professed Christians which is sociologically strong and fairly
authentic religiously, we can see that an effort has been made to
christianize the civilization. There seems to be an irrepressible
exigence: Christians have never accepted the restriction of their
activities to the sphere of religion. This was the case even in the
days of Julian the Apostate when he attempted to exclude them
from the function of teaching and to "send them back to their
Galilean Churches to comment Matthew and Luke" (Ep 61 C).
And they still cannot accept it today in the People's Democracies,
for instance, of Eastern Europe.

An historian would be the last person to deny the very real
influence exerted by the major religions and ideologies. It is common practice to speak of Buddhist, Zoroastrian (in the Sassanid
Empire) and Islamic civilizations or of Christian civilization in the
case of the *Spätantike* and the Western or Byzantine Middle Ages.
Of course it is necessary to define the exact significance of such a
term, but it cannot be denied that the influence was real and fruitful. True, there can be no common measure between the splendor
of Truth itself and the benefits it may have brought to the human
order. The latter can never be more than *epiphenomena*, given over
and above, if I may be permitted to transpose Aristotle's famous
formula onto this level. In its essence, Christianity is a religion
which exists for God and for his glory and not, first of all, to
provide an answer to our temporal problems—even if, in point of
fact, its influence does help to resolve them. Christianity is oriented

towards the building of the City of God; it is not first of all, nor specifically, designed to help us organize the earthly city. It is not a force for stirring up revolution (nor for preventing it, as advocates of law and order may be tempted to think). Its role is not to develop civilization or undermine it, as the pagan might suppose. But in fact it does exert an influence on civilization which may well prove to be decisive.

The theoretical mechanism of that action can readily be reconstructed. I attempted a sketch of such an analysis once before, in a book of my youth,[30] and I think that the best thing I can do here is simply to repeat it while trying to make it more accurate. Ordinarily speaking, Christianity does not create civilizations. This is not its purpose. In fact, however, history shows more than one instance in which Christianity has, if not given birth to, or created, a civilization, at least promoted the development of civilizations to a higher level. And this has happened because, if for no other reason, before the supernatural can be grafted onto a civilization, Christianity requires that man attain a minimum level of development in his own nature.

In particular, as a religion of the Book, Christianity requires a minimum level of literacy. This was the case amongst the peoples of the Middle East who were evangelized in the third and fourth centuries: Christianity gave a new lease of life to the ancient Egyptian and Aramaean cultures (whence the rich development of Coptic and Syriac literature) and stimulated the development of the national cultures of Ethiopia, Armenia and Georgia as well as among the Caucasian Iberians and the Goths of the Lower Danube. But normally Christianity is introduced into a civilization which is already established and which is bent on its proper temporal task of organizing human life on this earth. Christians, in their quality as men, benefit like all their fellows from the achievements of their civilization and take part in its tasks: "Even the heavenly

[30] H. I. Marrou, *Fondements d'une culture chrétienne*, Paris, Bloud & Gay, 1934 (Cahiers de la nouvelle journée).

city, therefore, while in its state of pilgrimage, avails itself of the peace of earth" (*City of God* XIX, 17).

The Church is not the world, but she lives in the world and occupies herself with her own sanctification of the world. She is represented by men and, having to act upon men, she cannot remain indifferent to the progress of the civilization in which history has placed her. She must pray for it, evangelize it, preach to it, rebuke it in season and out of season, make it wholesome (this was one of the meanings, if you remember, of the Gospel figure of the "Salt of the Earth"). Slowly, gradually, she exorcizes, baptizes and strengthens institutions and mores, or at least tries her utmost to do so, attempting to purify them of their intrinsically perverse components and adapt them to the exigencies of a normal Christian life. She does everything in her power to raise them above themselves and their own immediate ends to serve the spiritual end which she knows—and she is alone in knowing this fully—to be the ultimate end of man and of history.

I have been using the word "Church" for the sake of brevity and also because it is perfectly legitimate to use this word to designate the gathering of all those who are baptized and who live by the Spirit of Christ. I shall continue to use the term in this sense, but it is necessary, before going any further, to clarify any possible misunderstanding in the minds of my readers: for too many Christians the word "Church" evokes the strictly limited picture of ecclesiastical institutions and the hierarchical pyramid of its structure, in an unpleasantly clerical sense. Let us try and avoid this snare: normally (there was an exception due to a lack of culture, in the High Middle Ages in the West) it is not the Church as organized institution, it is not the hierarchical officials of the Church as such, who intervene and act in the name of the institutional Church or in the name of the hierarchy to influence the secular city, techniques and civilization. It is Christian men, formed in the spirit of the Gospel by that institution and by the ministry of its official representatives, who act upon the structures of civilization. They intervene personally and collectively (and, as we have seen,

they often act in disorganized ways and sometimes in direct contradiction to each other), as men amongst men, according to the
inspiration of their own consciences, their own judgments which
may be more or less autonomous, more or less well informed, more
or less authentically faithful to the ideal they profess. Here again
we are touching on the mystery of freedom.

But in the field of empirical history the good grain and the darnel
grow up together, inextricably intermixed, and thanks to the care
the Enemy bestows on it, the darnel is abundantly represented. The
structures of civilization, in most cases, do not stem directly from
Christianity, and Christianity has much to learn from men. Our
contemporaries are often very willing to emphasize the almost
systematic attitude of opposition that Christian circles seemed to
feel obliged to manifest toward the emergence of modern civilization
—from the philosophy of the Enlightenment to Stalinist politics or
current mores. The ideas, institutions and practices which arose in
reaction to the surviving remnants of mediaeval Christendom in
the Western world were automatically suspected, and most often
with good reason, of being an attack on Christianity itself while
presenting themselves as attacking only Christendom.

But an historian must also remember that throughout the centuries the attitude of the Church has always included a strongly
negative element (classical theology did not wait for the advent of
Kierkegaard to express its distrust with regard to the world). The
civilization of the High Roman Empire—Tertullian conveys this
very clearly—was not a favorable cultural environment for nascent
Christianity, but then neither were the Late Empire with its
totalitarian exigencies nor the High Middle Ages with its lack of
culture . . . (there is no point in pursuing this enumeration any
further).

Without positing this as a law that suffers few exceptions, we
may remark that it does often happen that the appearance of a
totally new phenomenon of civilization in the sphere of history
seems, at first sight, to bear the marks of Antichrist. I am not
speaking only of those cases in which the intellectual comfort of

Christian society has been upset and has taken fright too easily, seeing the shadow of Antichrist over everything new. The radical ambivalence of history means that everything is always very complex. I shall only attempt a very general picture of this question.

Is it not true that the history of the Church has been marked throughout the centuries by a succession of martyrs? The Church will always have to suffer and do battle before it can devote itself to the slow work of influence and transformation. And in its battles it can, for a time, be defeated, swept away and totally suppressed in any given period or geographical area. It is impossible to compare a map showing the extent of Christianity at the end of antiquity and one showing the spread of Islam since the Middle Ages without feeling a twinge of distress. How many bishoprics of the East are nothing more than empty titles in "the lands of the infidel."

At other times, when historical and sociological conditions are more favorable, this laborious work that goes on unremittingly is crowned with some success and ends by making a habitable dwelling out of the unhealthy, uncomfortable environment that was first imposed on the Christians. "Wash that which is soiled, heal that which is wounded, govern that which has gone astray": this can be applied not only to the Spirit but also to the Church—to Christians—in whom he lives, and not only to the work of sanctification but also to that of organizing man's temporary dwelling place, this "tent" (2 Co 5:1). Civilizations develop throughout the ages by virtue of the complex web of causalities that we have attempted to define: Christianity takes its place within this network and seeks to influence it.

I have all too often heard this tendency reviled as though Christians allowed themselves to be carried away on the stream of history—but the objection was always voiced by adversaries who had forgotten the specifically supernatural mission of the Church and who were overly concerned with the role that it plays, or could play, in the fields of force influencing secular history. This is far from being a true picture! Christians struggle desperately, or they die, crushed. At least this is how they should behave. It is only too obvious that they have often shown themselves unfaithful to their mission and this is infinitely deplorable but an historian should not be surprised by it. His very function disabuses him, accustomed as he is to record the ravages and wiles of sin.

There is often a good deal of weariness mixed with our human inadequacy, in the face of this Sisyphean task. New problems keep coming up, and with them new trials and difficulties, just when earlier problems seemed to be on the point of being resolved and the situation seemed to be getting bearable (or, at least, one had become used to it!). In 1791, the European Church was on the side of the kings, at whose hands she had suffered so much when they were called Hohenstaufen or Philip the Fair. Today she has taken up the defense of the very same human rights which she combated so vigorously in the nineteenth century (however one should compare the different contexts: in the heyday of Liberalism they were posited in opposition to the rights of God; today they constitute the last ditch stand of personalism against the onslaught of pagan neo-totalitarianism).

If I were inclined to be conservative I could explain this behavior which Christians have so frequently manifested in history by saying that they are naturally more sensitive to the good that is in danger of being lost and to the evil that must be tolerated than to the still uncertain improvements that innovators claim to pursue. But as I am not a conservative, my function is to denounce the sophistry that has all too often allowed men who cling to law and order to close their eyes to the scandal of established disorder which is nothing less than piracy with a veneer of legality. I fully endorse the arguments that Mounier marshalled in defense of this theme more than thirty years ago. As St. Augustine puts it, "Justice being taken away, then what are kingdoms but great robberies?" (*City of God* IV, 4). Think, for instance, of those bishops who fled from France in 1790, and who wrote pastoral letters to the faithful explaining that the Christian religion was inseparable from the monarchy. They too easily forgot that the system with which they proclaimed their solidarity had entrusted the diocese of Strasbourg to the Prince de Rohan who was involved in the scandal of the Queen's necklace and the diocese of Autun to Talleyrand!

Of course, as her most urgent duty is to pray, to preach and to proclaim the Gospel, the Church as an institution will always accommodate herself easily to any fairly stable system, just so long as she has room to breathe. She will leave to the jurists the task of distinguishing between the established powers and legitimate power . . . It is not essential to her work in history, which is to promote holiness. Unfortunately, since most of the saints remain unknown to the world, and since there are many sinners in the Church, her spiritual countenance can only be seen by the eyes of faith and prophets will always be needed within the Church. Their uncomfortable function is to denounce the scandal of the presence in the world of men who are Christian only in name, who are in league with evil and profit from it if only by their own passivity, being all too comfortable in its company. The vocation of a prophet calls, certainly, for a special charisma, but all of us can begin to exercise this function for ourselves and with regard to ourselves— for, to quote a wise nun,[31] I am the only mission-country to which I can be quite certain that I am mandated to bring the Gospel.

38. THE GREATNESS OF THE MIDDLE AGES

But everything we have said so far has been very general and is, therefore, still a little theoretical. In point of fact when we discuss the possibilities and limitations of a Christian civilization we never do so without referring implicitly or explicitly to the prime example offered by mediaeval Latin Christendom. (The discussion would be

[31] Geneviève Galois, *La vie du petit saint Placide*, Paris, 1954, p. 64.

more fruitful if we also took into consideration the no less typical
example of oriental Christendom, both Byzantine and post-
Byzantine, but it is not well enough known, except by the specialists,
and moreover it does not have the same direct relationship with the
civilization of today.)

Western thinking seems to be almost obsessed by the lingering
memory of those centuries of Christendom. We never seem to have
finished burying this noble corpse, we are for ever making declara-
tions to the effect that the parenthesis opened by Constantine—or
Charlemagne—is now closed. It is not only Christians who do this,
but the question has been more pressing for them. To put things
very crudely: the West was originally pagan, it became Christian,
and this gave birth to the civilization of the Middle Ages, which
was a relatively successful accomplishment but which eventually
miscarried, and ever since we have been cleaning up the debris.

It is very true that within the last few centuries (Bossuet already
had this attitude) the action of Christians, especially in the political
sphere, has been largely aimed at defending and maintaining at all
costs anything that could be salvaged in the way of institutions or
customs which the Middle Ages had stamped with a Christian
imprint and which stood in danger of being swept away by the
emergence of a modern civilization hostile or simply foreign to the
Faith. Christians have spent tremendous sums of energy in these
prolonged rear-guard actions, often imbued with a hopeless spirit
of resignation, and this has also contributed notably to that paling of
eschatological hope which we have already denounced and has given
the impression to those outside the Church that the Christian faith
was in some way bound up with the restoration, the conservation,
the memory of a phase of civilization which appears, objectively, to
be over.

I do not deny that such holding-actions are still going on in Italy,
Quebec, Spain, and Ireland in an attempt to preserve the officially
Christian character of civil society. Even in France some isolated
sociological communities exist which are so homogeneous on the
religious level that one can be justified in speaking of Christendoms.

And there are and will always be nostalgic Christians who continue to look to the past. . . . But I am writing on the hypothesis that these are regressive phenomena and that the real problem which faces us is the problem of a Christian minority, an unvanquished minority, it is true and one more than ever conscious of its missionary nature, but nevertheless a minority which now lives in the midst of a society that has been radically dechristianized. This is a difficult situation to assume but, at least on a theoretical level, it gives us complete independence when it comes to forming an objective diagnosis of the Middle Ages considered as a Christian civilization.

I have lived long enough, by now, to have seen three different types of interpretations applied to the Middle Ages which, far from contradicting or voiding each other, are complementary, like the successive strokes of the brush touching up a painting. At first there was the position which we inherited from the early days of the Romantic period—in France, exemplified by Chateaubriand and his *Génie du Christianisme*. In view of my earlier strictures on this work, I must at this point emphasize its very real historical importance and the permanent value of the thesis it sets out to defend: in face of the scorn poured on Christianity by the philosophy of the Enlightenment, and nurtured as he was by neo-classical prejudice and a hatred for non-Christians, Chateaubriand set out to demonstrate that "religion"—and especially the Christian religion—was not synonymous with "barbarism" (one remembers the phrase with which Gibbon summed up his *Decline and Fall of the Roman Empire,* "I have described the triumph of barbarism and religion"). It was important to rediscover that the Middle Ages had its own forms of greatness and that it had contributed to the great masterpieces that constitute mankind's heritage. The cathedrals of Vézelay, Chartres and Amiens are "places where perfection dwells" as surely as the Acropolis. It is small-minded to object that even though our cathedrals are beautiful "they are not solidly built and they fall to ruin in five or six-hundred years." After all, they stood up very well to the bombings of World War One (those that took place during the Second World War seem to have been more selective), and what if the nave of Beauvais did fall down because it was too ambitious? The pillars of the giant temples of Selinonte are also scattered over the ground. . . .

In the 1920's admiration for the Middle Ages reached new heights. First its art and poetry, and then the originality of its thinking had been discovered (although it is not strictly correct, the term "Mediaeval philosophy" was widely used) and it was recognized that it had played an important role in the elaboration of material techniques opening the way to what was to become modern science. But what we most admired was the fact that it provided us with an observable instance of what we called, using a Platonic term, "a healthy civilization (*Rep.* II, 372e). Sorokin's analysis assigned to it the inelegant term of "socio-cultural super-system"— that is, a whole civilization organized around one conception of the world and of life, a *Lebens-und-Weltanschauung,* a common ideal and reason for living, a principle of unity to which all techniques, institutions, ways of thinking or feeling, were subordinated as to their higher end. Toward 1925 this was what we admired most in the Middle Ages: the ideal of an organically coherent civilization in which every man, whether he be

> *King, politician, monk, craftsman or chemist,*
> *Architect, soldier, doctor, lawyer,*

had his assigned place, his function to fill, in full communion with all other men. What a contrast with the "anarchy of values" in the world in which we were living! Christians were not the only ones at that time to yearn for the Middle Ages. In 1927–1928 Waldo Frank, one of the group of American cultural critics of the *New Republic,* measured the decomposition of European culture by comparing it to the society in which Dante lived, in which everything fell logically into place around a central core. From God to the priest, from the Emperor to the serf, from Heaven to Hell, from the star to the atom, from good to evil, everything was integrated and Dante lived on the same footing as his own cook!

If non-Christians yearned for the Middle Ages, how much more so the Christians who were obliged to live in a world that was becoming more and more uncomfortable for them. A few obstinate survivals from the time of Christendom, like the shreds of a once glorious mantle, were not enough to conceal the tragic nakedness of the facts: Western civilization had reverted to a paganism as spontaneous as that of the Roman world of the first three centuries. "The small remnant" had been tried and purified as though by fire, but it was so "small" that all of us felt ourselves forced to a heartrending revision of the forms of life that our times offered us: It was only natural that we should dream of a new Middle Ages.

But Berdiaev's choice of the title *Un nouveau Moyen Age* for his book, written in 1923, was in one way unfortunate. Nothing in history ever happens all over again. However, Berdiaev was not thinking of some vain attempt at restoration of a past that had already been abolished but of another civilization that could become, as the Middle Ages had attempted to be, a Christian civilization. A civilization in which man would not be faced with the heroic task of reacting alone, or almost alone, against the overpowering influence of his environment but in which personal life and culture could develop normally in a favorable atmosphere, spontaneously in harmony with the collective patterns of thought and feeling, with the prevailing institutions and mores. It is never comfortable, nor easy nor healthy, to be a minority of outsiders. In view of the ravages of sin and our human weakness, the human race yields a very small harvest, statistically speaking, whether in holiness or in genius. And so it is easy to see the advantages, for the Church, of being well established sociologically and demographically. Without ten centuries of Umbrian Christianity behind them could St. Francis and Franciscanism have ever come to flower? If the Reconquest of Spain had not happened, St. John of the Cross would have been a Sufi.

39. THE LIMITATIONS OF THE MIDDLE AGES

But the years have gone by and we are further than ever from conditions which permit us to glimpse a civilization of Christian inspiration. In the meantime the emergence and, alas, the experience of totalitarian systems have taught us that the will to impose a unity of inspiration and structure on the city of man can lead to monstrous caricatures (compared with this tyranny, the anarchy of values seems a lesser evil). In this context we seem to have come to a third phase in our appreciation of mediaeval Christendom. We have become more aware of its failures. No indeed, the Christian city was not the kingdom of God. From the beginning I have denounced the illusion—and even the neo-millenarist heresy—inherent in men's hope of animating all expressions of the temporal order with the spirit of the Gospel and, so to speak, of signing everything with the Cross.

We must now judge the Middle Ages, not on its theology, but on the properly human level, insofar as it was an attempt to bring into being what we have called a "healthy civilization." Taking the hint from our own experience of men and fallen human nature, we can well imagine what sheep-like conformism, sociological pressure and implicit violence to the consciences of individuals was necessarily implied by the realization of near-unanimity in mediaeval society.

As far as the origins of this society go, we only have to consult the Fathers: they were the contemporaries of the unexpected growth of a society that was nominally Christian, following on the conversion of the Emperors and, thence, of the Empire. They were not fooled by the swelling crowds in the churches, overflowing like the nets of the miraculous catch of fish and, like that catch, a very mixed bag: "poor in holiness, rich in sin." And St. Augustine remarked with melancholy that as the prestige of Christianity became better established, hypocrisy could be seen to thrive (*Enarr. in Ps.* 7, 9; in Ps. 30, 2, II, 2). As for the Middle Ages properly speaking, they were rife with violence in the most brutal sense of the word. Violence was openly used on the unyielding minorities, in the attempt to subdue or get rid of them, whether it was a question of the surviving remnants of Judaism or the emerging groups such as the Cathari and the Waldenses—at the beginning, these unfortunate people asked nothing better than to remain within Christendom as a leaven of purification and interior reform. Violence was also used in the mission to the outside world: Oh, those Knights of the Sword, the Brotherhood of soldiers for Christ! I know very well that the Slav and Baltic peoples, to say nothing of the Muslims, were not always very easy to convert, but there is great difference between recognizing this and considering it as quite normal to associate the sword with the Cross! Again and again we find the same impatience and inability to tolerate the delays imposed by God's patience which led to a veritable rape of history, under the pretext of hastening the Parousia.

This should be enough to put us on our guard against being too optimistic in our interpretation of Western mediaeval Christendom. It should have been more Christian in quantity and in quality than any other society simply because of the historical accident that gave it birth: the collapse of the civilization of the Late Roman Empire under the onslaught of the Germanic invasion.

Of course, even if they were barbarians, the invaders brought with them elements of civilization—material techniques (as, for instance the high degree of perfection they had reached in tempering steel), legal traditions, their own forms of sensibility—but they were disparate values and they were often only in an embryonic stage of development.

In the same way the heritage of classical civilization had not entirely disappeared and the Christian religion, in particular, was the most vigorous of the elements that had survived. In the midst of this chaotic situation Christianity appeared as the only life-principle around which the renascent civilization could structure itself. In the beginning, even though many elements of the antique heritage had been preserved, very often this was so only to the extent to which Christianity had adopted and preserved them for its own service. For example, the reason why Latin and, thereby the art of writing, was not lost during these dark days—it could well have happened: Coptic Egypt had lost the secret of the hieroglyphs—was quite simply because it had become the only liturgical language of the West.

This accounts for the characteristic flavor of the Western Middle Ages which were not only Christian but ecclesiastical or, rather, clerical, especially in comparison with their contemporary counterpart, the Byzantine Middle Ages which were no less imbued with the sacred but which, with the Empire, had retained the bipolar structure of the civilization of later antiquity. The Church was one of the poles, but opposite the Church stood the Emperor, heir to an unbroken tradition handed down from Augustus and Diocletian and a whole system of properly secular values which, even when Christianized, had preserved their autonomy; first and foremost amongst them being an autonomous culture based on the works of Homer (the West was, one day, to rediscover Virgil).

The weakening and disappearance of temporal institutions explains the compensatory function that the ecclesiastical institutions were forced to assume during the Middle Ages. The whole of our educational system—from the village school to the university—stems from the school system established by the Church for its own needs (formation of the clergy). The fact that the word "cleric" also meant someone who was literate seems paradoxical today, but at that time there was no culture that was not religious. And this did not apply only to letters and the arts! Churchmen had to turn their hand to everything from foreign politics to public works: Thus St. Didier, Bishop of Cahors from 630 to 655, undertook to install a water supply in his episcopal see and applied to his colleague, the Bishop of Clermont, to find qualified workers (Ep. II, 14).

It is only fair to note in passing that several functions which are now considered as belonging to the secular city—such as are now filled by Welfare and Social Security—were not assumed by the

Church only to compensate for a lack in civil society; they spring from the spirit of the Gospel, the ideal of *agape,* and have grown up in the shadow of the Cross. Hospitals, hostels, asylums were all, originally, Christian institutions and had no equivalent in the civilizations of antiquity.

But apart from these exceptional examples one cannot say that the Church created (in the participatory sense in which it can truly be said that a human work has been created out of nothing) the elements of mediaeval civilization. Its function was to try and christianize those elements, and this was not always easy: as an extenuating factor in the lack of success one must take into account the immensity of the task. Once again we encounter the autonomy of the specifically technical domain and the internal logic that governs its development.

At the risk of contradicting a certain superficial school of apologetics I must declare that it was not Christianity that gave rise to the agrarian and social structures which did away with slavery in favor of serfdom and then, gradually, lightened the yoke of serfdom. What a complex tangle of things, here! The fact that the term "Slav" came to mean slave (the word was used as early as 937 in this sense in a Latin diploma of the Emperor Otto 1st) is a sign of that infamous sore on the flesh of mediaeval Christendom which allowed the pagans to be deprived of the basic human rights it recognized for its own offspring. The first to suffer were the victims of the raids carried out amongst the Slav tribes who showed resistance to being evangelized, and an extremely profitable trade developed by shipping them to the Arabs of Spain and the East. The practice continued with Muslim prisoners of the Iberian *Reconquista* and, later, with the Corsair wars, spread to the whole of the Mediterranean area (even the Eastern Christians, Greek, Russian and Georgian, were not spared). Slavery therefore never really disappeared from the legal horizon of the Christians of the West, and this was all too evident when, at the end of the fifteenth century, the colonization of the Americas opened the way to a horrible resurgence of the traffic in slaves.

But it is not permissible, except for the sake of analysis and argument, to isolate a social system from the human reality that constitutes it and to which it gives shape. Christianity could not abandon the men and the personal and collective destinies that were involved in the very existence of a system. And so we see the Church intervening in every area to combat sin to make the exercise of Christian virtues possible or at least a little less difficult, to humanize barbarian mores and bring peace to men's hearts. In short, the Church sought to Christianize the institutions of society at the risk—and the risk became almost an inevitability once Christians were no longer shut up in their ghettos—of enrolling the faithful in a feudal system. This explains the periodic necessity for inner reforms that constantly needed to be renewed, that were always imperfect and all too often postponed. I wonder if it has been sufficiently recognized that Luther's revolt followed only a few months after the failure, in regard to the reform of ecclesiastical mores, of the Fifth Ecumenical Council of the Lateran (the Council ended on March 16, 1517, the theses of Wittemberg were made public on November 1st).

An historian cannot deny that this effort of Christianization was carried out with great perseverance and sincerity and that it was very successful in more than one instance. Europe still experiences some of the benefits of it today. The action that was undertaken with a view to limiting the ravages of war and making it more human—if it is possible to speak of "humanizing" war—that led to the Geneva Convention (now fast becoming a dead letter) began with recommendations formulated in the Councils and with legislation in favor of peace, the Peace of God or the Truce of God, by which the mediaeval Church sought to bring about a more human order in a world of violence and savagery.

In all fairness one cannot close one's eyes to the successes that were obtained, however partial and precarious they may have been. We should react against the cynicism of a sociologist who is tempted to draw the conclusion that as soon as any of the great religions becomes a mass phenomenon, the faithful pick and choose amongst the prescriptions that they will abide by and retain only those that do not inhibit their fundamental passions and spontaneous behavior. Of course one can see why they arrive at such pessimistic conclusions: the civilizing work of the Church which gives rise to Christendom is not strictly the work of the Church as we have defined it, based on its holiness—the Church as an integral part of the City of God—but rather the result of the practical behavior of the sociological mass of the faithful, amongst whom, I must repeat, there are always more sinners than saints, which opposes the whole weight of its inertia in obstinate resistance to the teaching of its Doctors or the initiatives of its spiritual elite. In addition to this there is the inertia which arises on the purely technical level: just as matter cannot easily be conquered and manipulated by the hand of the artist, in the same way a given technique cannot easily be turned from the path of its spontaneous orientation, its own specific goal, and be penetrated and remodeled from within by a religious ideal. And so, to come back to the problem of war, much effort has been expended in vain to combat the implacable logic of the arms race: there have been an impressive number of condemnations uttered against inhuman weaponry throughout the evolution that has led civilization to the age of chemical warfare and the atom bomb: in 1139 the Second Lateran Council condemned the crossbow and even the bow as cruel and deadly weapons!

40. THE CHRISTIAN CITY AND THE KINGDOM OF GOD

It is not at all surprising, therefore, that mediaeval Christendom was imperfect and incomplete. In the effort to make it an authentically Christian civilization there was so much foot-dragging and procrastination, so many concessions to human weakness made through lassitude and weariness. It is even less to be wondered at if one considers the time element: the *tempo,* the pace, at which history moves is so much more rapid than the pace of evolution in the Darwinian sense of the term. Evolution in this sense has almost unlimited time at its disposal for the work of adapting and transforming the species. The history of civilization moves much faster. This can be seen very clearly in the case of mediaeval Christendom: the Christianizing of an institution, a mental category or a behavioral pattern had hardly been achieved—sometimes, indeed, was hardly begun—before the spontaneous transformation of techniques elicited new, unexpected problems which completely changed the elements of the situation.

The effort to Christianize feudal customs and the brutal mores of a warrior class was carried on until the end of the Middle Ages. Perseverance sometimes met with success—instanced in the rites of chivalry—and sometimes with failure: Council after Council condemned the danger and cupidity involved in the sport of jousting in vain. This effort was still going on when, at the turn of the eleventh and twelfth centuries, the new ideal of courtly love arose with all the glamor of its ostentatious display of nobility, the exalting of women as mediators of the absolute, the ideal of love, the Romances . . . And the work of Christianization began all over again, leading to the Quest for the Holy Grail and the *Vita Nuova.*

But before long other problems arose, and these were not so easily resolved: the development of national monarchies and the modern idea of nationhood was to offend the feeling that men still cherished of belonging to the Christian Republic. The resurgence of Roman Law at Bologna in the beginning of the twelfth century marked a modern renascence of the old pagan idol of the sovereign State and provided new arms in the struggle against the Churchmen, Frederick II's lawyers and, later, Philip the Fair. At the same time, an economy built on trade was rapidly laying the foundations of the capitalistic system.

In the face of these innovations Christianity certainly did not remain passive. To mention only her reaction to the latter development, we can still appreciate, today, her vigorous response to the new idol of Profit, expressed by her obstinate condemnation of money-lending for interest which was considered to be usurious. Many instances, from Charlemagne's *Admonitio generalis,* in 789, to the Bull, *Vix pervenit,* published by Benedict XIV in 1745, can legitimately be seen as proof that the will to remain faithful to the Gospel ideal was still at work. On the other hand we also have to admit that this long struggle was, on the practical level, ineffectual because the spokesmen for the Church lacked competence on the specifically technical level. What was needed was a totally different mentality, conceptualizations better adapted to the situation (when Capitalism was, so obviously, triumphant, it was no use repeating the old Aristotelian adage: "money is not, of itself, profitable"), and a greater awareness of the proper structures of the economic order.

Thus Christendom began to disintegrate: even those elements that had been successfully established as valid and holy began to show signs of decadence. One instance of this was scholastic theology: one only has to remember the atmosphere of decadent nominalism in which the young Luther was formed—or misformed. A distressing contrast grew up between the ideal of Christendom which continued to be elaborated ever more consciously on the theoretical plane and the reality that conformed less and less to the theory.

Never had Christendom been more clearly conceived of and developed as a notional and institutional system than in the beginning of the fourteenth century. This was especially true of the great neo-Thomistic theologians of the Hermits of St. Augustine, the advisers of Boniface VIII who aided him in writing the Bull *Unam Sanctum* (November 18, 1302), which was so bitterly challenged by history less than one year later at Anagni (September 7, 1303). A little later, in 1365, Andrea da Firenze began the frescoes in the Spanish chapel of Santa Maria Novella. One of these paintings is a magnificent picture of the ideal schema of Christendom: twin thrones on which are seated the Pope and the Emperor are set against the background of the Church. The Emperor, imitated by the princes, magistrates and judges who surround him, holds his great sword ready for the service of the spiritual power. On the right of the Pope stand the Cardinals, Bishops and Religious of all Orders; on the edges of this group stands the pack of God's hounds, the *domini canes:* one of them is busy refuting the arguments of the heretics, another is seen converting some Jews, etc. How beautifully orderly it all is! And during this very period, 1365–1370, the Hundred Years War has flared up again, the Empire in the person of Charles IV has retreated to Germany, the union with the Greeks has foundered, the Pope is wavering between Avignon and Rome, in England Wycliff and the Lollards are in revolt against the law of the Church, ushering in the series of modern heresies . . .

Should we conclude, then, that Western Christendom was, in the final accounting, a failure? Yes. It failed utterly in respect to the ideal of Christian civilization it had aimed at. However, in all fairness it must be measured in the scale of human success or failure: all the works of man, including the most ambitious work of all, civilization, are destined to fail. There is no such thing as full success in secular history. Our wise men have always known this. Elaborating on a disillusioned reflection in Hamlet, Sainte-Beuve wrote: "In reality, people's dreams, plans and hopes always make me think of a regiment of fresh troops sent out in the morning to climb a long, steep defile, between two rows of archers, invisible and inevitable, who are lying in wait for them. If, by evening, the officer leading the attack and one or two ragged battalions managed to get through to the next city on the road with a semblance of a flag flying, it is called a victory . . ."

41. THE FAILURE OF ALL CIVILIZATION

Our analysis of the Middle Ages can furnish a framework for the study of any of the other great civilizations of history. All of them, without exception, have failed. All of them have begun to disintegrate before ever being brought to completion. All of them have felt the weight of the curse laid on the Tower of Babel: this is one of the major lessons to be drawn from the Biblical episode. Every great civilization is an attempt to bring about, here and now, on earth and within secular history an image, an essay, a beginning of the City of God. At the same time, it is a temptation—which, in the long run, men always give way to—to identify the type with the proto-type, the secular city with the City of God, as though man's destiny could be accomplished on this earth, as though his history could reach total fulfillment and meaning within the dimension of time. Every earthly city—and we must proclaim this openly even if we are not in a position to analyze it fully—is a volatile mixture of Jerusalem and Babylon, of the City of God and the city of evil: "the two cities are still inextricably intertwined" . . . People have often been scandalized by the negative judgment implied in the term "earthly city" when it comes from the vivid pen of St. Augustine. It is obvious that, in essence the "earthly city," the secular city, is not a reality to be condemned: it is the normal context of the human condition. It is the ground in which humanity is meant to flourish and it was created and blessed by God: "Be fruitful, multiply, fill the earth and conquer it" (Gn 1:28); it is the land on which we cultivate the talents that have been entrusted to us. It is not beyond the powers of man to conceive the theoretical model of a city in which justice, order and peace reign, in which peace is ordered to the creation and utilization of all those values that go to make up what we call civilization or culture, those goods that are adapted to our human condition, the indispensable realities of our temporal life: this is the lesson that stands out so clearly in Book XIX of the *City of God* (see especially chapters 13, 14 and 17).

But we must add immediately that this can only be a purely theoretical picture or, if you prefer, an ideal projection indicating the goal that all action should strive to reach (we shall see in a moment just what restrictions are implied by the words, "if you prefer"). Such a blue-print corresponds to no reality available to our empirical observation, either in our own life-experience or in history.

If such a plan were, in fact, within the realm of possibility, man's temporal work would be a direct contribution to the development and the coming of the City of God, for everything that has any value—since every specifically human value contains an element of absolute value—can be saved and integrated in the eternal. But we have to concede that what actually exists is not simply nature in its natural goodness as it was willed by a good Creator. In history we also have to deal with vitiated nature, nature that has been deformed and weakened by sin.

In point of fact we can see all around us the obstinate and multiform presence of sin and evil. The curve described by human activity can only be identified for one brief instant with the trajectory of the ideal path that would have led it directly to God. All those who have first-hand experience of a war of liberation or independence can bear me out: have they not always brought away with them this distressing, ambivalent experience? The original thrust of the ideal that fired them was centered on attaining an absolute good, their primary intention was pure: they refused an alienation that had become literally un-bearable, intolerable. They espoused the impassioned claim to personal and human dignity. But even before victory had been won—and although it had already been paid for by so much pain, blood and tears—it was tainted and corrupted by useless and cruel violence, by greedy ambition and self-seeking . . . And what of the bitter taste of victory once it has been won?

Man always succumbs to his own concupiscence, and justice in the city gives way to the will to power; peace is only the triumph of force; so-called order is based not on harmony and love but on "established disorder." All the goods and values of this earth, whether they go by the name of country, art, or science, are set up as ultimate ends whereas they should be treated only as intermediate ends, as steps in man's ascent to God, as transparent realities through which and by means of which man reaches the ultimate transcendence. And so these values and blessings become corrupt even in their very essence. They are simply monstrous caricatures of what they could have been if we had used them properly.

It would be a mistake to jump to the conclusion that this is the professional pessimism of an historian. It is a fact: everywhere he sees the victory of sin, evil triumphing over the forces of good. The secular city, seen empirically, is a mockery of what it could be and was often intended to be: a foreshadowing of the City of God. In collective history we meet with exactly the same experience of failure as, on the moral level, in the personal life: "In fact this seems to be the rule, that every single time I want to do good it is something evil that comes to hand" (Rm 7:21).

For someone my age this view of history is not simply the result of theoretical speculation, it is the bitter fruit of experience. We have lived long enough to have learned a little more than our fathers before us. The contribution of our generation to the store of common wisdom could be phrased thus: "We civilizations, we now know *why* we are mortal." History is a cemetery of dead civilizations, or rather a cemetery of still-born civilizations, of inchoative development that has been prematurely interrupted, of social and political forms and cultures in an embryonic state which were destroyed before reaching their full flowering. History is the burial place of finished products that have betrayed the promise of their youth, of teratological mutations, of monstrous senescence.

The story of every great civilization is the story of a process that has failed to reach fulfillment. In the beginning there is the raw material furnished by whatever stage of development has been reached by the spontaneous evolution of techniques. (As we have seen, this development lies, for the most part, outside the power of man's initiative and control.) An ideal which is more or less unconscious to begin with, and which later becomes explicit, seeks to harness these techniques and to shape them according to its own demands, endeavoring, at the same time, to unify them. But this unity appears more as a horizon toward which one moves. No one can ever flatter himself he has reached it! The holistic hypothesis that sees civilization as a whole whose parts are mutually dependent is purely notional, but it is a perennial temptation for one who has a deep-seated aversion for the indefinite and the multiple, as though this were synonymous with unintelligibility.

History shows that a civilization is an ideal that has never been

fully and completely realized. Rather, as time goes on one becomes
more and more conscious of the widening gap between what is
actually accomplished in a civilization and the ideal plan conceived
by its elite. The mental picture becomes more and more perfect in
every detail whilst the reality continues to refuse to incarnate it. We
saw this in the case of the mediaeval West, and the same phenomenon can be observed in all the other cases that fall within the scope
of our knowledge of the past. A civilization will always be an abortive undertaking, that begins to disintegrate before it is even completed. At the beginning it is always a beautiful dream and a noble
undertaking, but as the theoretical picture becomes clearer and
clearer, the dichotomy we spoke of begins to show itself between
what men would like to be and what, in fact, they remain or become. Then the day comes when this discrepancy becomes too great
and, the whole structure hopelessly off-balance, it begins to keel
over and, like Proust's old man, totters on the long stilts of its
past . . .

42. ROME AND LIBERAL EUROPE

I shall not venture to follow in Toynbee's footsteps and attempt to
show how this law can be applied to all the twenty-one (or however many they may be) great civilizations mentioned in the cata-
logues of history. I would simply like to evoke two instances, other
than that of mediaeval Christendom, about which I can claim some
knowledge: Imperial Rome and the modern liberal civilization which
is our direct forebear.

First of all Rome: the plan to unify the whole of the civilized
world and establish one community embracing all civilized men, the
only ones who could rightly be called men . . . this was no mean
dream. However, in order to identify the Mediterranean Empire

with the *oikoumen*—the earth inhabited by men worthy of the name—the Romans had to ignore the awkward fact of their Persian neighbors living on the other side of the Euphrates—this was one of the first lies and the root of much hypocrisy—and yet the Iranian Empire was also a highly civilized State and, like Rome, heir to the great work of Alexander.

Rome had united nations that had formerly been enemies into one Fatherland and subjected them less to the domination of a conqueror than to the rule of law. Order, peace and prosperity reigned. "The good life" was universally acknowledged—however diverse they might be, hellenistic philosophies all agreed on this point—as the highest value, the reason for living, the ideal to be striven for. It was a human ideal, too human perhaps from a Christian point of view, but it was capable of mustering great reserves of human energy and enthusiasm.

It is perhaps hardly necessary to recall the famous *Panegyric* of Rome pronounced in 143 by Aelius Aristides the rhetorician, before the worthy Emperor Antoninus? The Empire is portrayed as living in harmony like a choir singing in unison without one false note or like a well-tuned instrument: "The whole world is celebrating. It has laid aside its armor of steel and abandoned itself freely to the beauty and the joy of living. The cities have all renounced their old rivalries or rather they are all fired by the same spirit of emulation: that of being the most beautiful and the most full of charm. Everywhere can be seen gymnasiums, fountains, propylaea, temples, workships, schools . . ." (*Or.* 26 K, 97).

Unfortunately this was only true of a small elite of which Aelius Aristides was the spokesman, a thin layer at the top of the social pyramid. In this civilization dominated exclusively by the urban aristocracy, these blessings, although they were very real, benefited only a few. They were inaccessible to the vast masses of the slaves and the poor—the *humiliores* for whom even the law was beginning to make itself a hard task-master. And the farther they were from the civilizing influence of the cities—permanent showcases of the blessings of the Pax Romana—the more hopelessly were the rural masses condemned to stagnate in primitive agricultural techniques which had hardly changed since the neolithic period.

On the other hand, beyond the frontiers of the Empire, the influence of Roman civilization was felt hardly at all or very sporadically by the Barbarians. With perfect ingenuousness, in the security of his own clear conscience, Aelius Aristides praises the Pax Romana and speaks of Ares, the God of the armies, being reduced to executing his war dance on the banks of the rivers that marked the borders of the Empire—the Rhine, the Danube and the Euphrates—which only means, in everyday language, that the soldiers at the outposts along the border were busy keeping the Barbarians at a distance . . . The day was to come when it was no longer possible to stand up against this pressure and the frontiers were overrun: the West stood by passively, or even actively assisted in the onslaught of this foreign proletariat (to use Toynbee's expression). We have the testimony of Salvian for fifth century Gaul and of St. Gregory the Great for Italy during the Lombard invasion: many of those who had never known anything but the overwhelming yoke of fiscal, police and political tyranny in the Imperial civilization went over to the Barbarians. They had had to pay too high a price to guarantee the "happiness" of the few . . .

It is the same story for the "civilization" of the Liberal period— say from 1776 to 1789 to 1914—I will not venture any further. It is all too obvious, today, that there was a great deal of illusion in their philosophy of progress. These men did not give much credence to original sin and many of their failures and false positions can be explained by the fact that they deliberately ignored this factor, which is one of the elements most essential to the analysis of the human condition. However I cannot bring myself to despise or underestimate the aspirations that were incarnate in the American Declaration of Rights or in that of the French Constituent Assembly.

It is true that this ideology stemming from the Enlightenment had developed quite separately from what remained of mediaeval, Christian Europe—some of which was totally obsolescent, some of which, however, remained perfectly valid—and so Christians usually saw "Liberalism" as a dangerous rival and, for more than a century, it was considered the principal enemy. In view of the circumstances this misunderstanding was inevitable, but it was also tragic: we can see this very clearly now that we are faced with the far more radical atheism of the totalitarian peril. The political philosophy of these first revolutionaries was only the echo of a certain number of elementary truths basic to all Christian thought.

Their impassioned pleading for the absolute and inalienable rights of man is based, ultimately, on the recognition of the fundamental notion of the human person, product of a special creative will and object of God's special love. "Article I: All men are born and remain free and equal in their rights; social distinctions can only be founded on the common good." There is no mistaking the echo of the scholastic teaching concerning the primary value of the common good. Liberty is conceived as resistance to oppression, a rejection of injustice. Equality: is it not the fundamental quality of the children of God and a projection in the civil order, of St. Paul's religious teaching: "and in that image there is no room for distinction between Greek and Jew, between the circumcised and the uncircumcised, or between Barbarian and Scythian, slave and free man—or between men and women—there is only Christ" (Col 3:11); and all this should normally flower in Fraternity.

I do not deny that these principles have inspired many really effective reforms at different times . . . but what an abyss between the ideal and the application! One does not have to be a Marxist to denounce the false claims of a purely formal liberty and a theoretical equality that have been drained of all real substance by the power of the almighty Dollar and the weight of economic and social conventions. As a theory that claimed to be founded on reason and, therefore, universally applicable, Liberalism should have been capable of promoting brotherhood amongst the nations. In fact we have witnessed just the opposite: the exacerbation of national conflicts which led the civilized States of Europe to a suicidal world war. And finally, the ingenuous identification of Western culture and civilization itself explains the perfectly clear conscience with which the same nations carried out their colonial enterprise and, under humanitarian pretexts, enslaved the Third World.

In this instance history confirms our own, personal experience: we have at last opened our eyes to the dichotomy that has gradually grown more and more pronounced between the sacred principles, so "simple and incontrovertible," proclaimed as the guiding principles of our civilization and what, in fact, that civilization still was— or had become all over again. We are in a position to take stock of the unconscious hypocrisy that was the bulwark of the ruling classes of the rich countries. The most flagrant manifestation of this hypocrisy is the Universal Declaration of the Rights of Man adopted by the United Nations on December 10, 1948 and which proclaims these same Liberal principles at a moment when it had already become quite obvious that men blithely refuse to abide by them, thus betraying the partial progress accomplished in the 19th Century (at least the USSR under Stalin, Ibn Saoud's Arabia and the South African racists had the elementary honesty to refuse to sign it). Article V of this document states: "No one shall be subjected to torture or to cruel, inhuman or degrading treatment or punishments." And yet, even before we had learned that torture was being used once again in the Soviet Union or in the French colonial wars, American literature had already taught us about "the third degree." If we revert to inquisitorial methods and try to obtain confessions as conclusive proof of guilt, we will necessarily be led to use such things.

43. A THEOLOGY OF FREEDOM

The rock of Sisyphus, Penelope's tapestry, the bottomless urn of the daughters of Danaüs: all these myths and images in the classical tradition echo the Biblical story of the curse of Babel. The wisdom of disillusionment illustrates the laborious and frustrating work of building a civilization. It is a task that is never done, that always has to be begun anew. This conviction, which we gain from a study of historical experience, would be very bitter indeed if we did not also know that true history is being realized, concealed within these vicissitudes, abortive attempts, betrayals and failures; if we did not know that, in spite of what appears on the surface, nothing of men's work and pain is ever really lost and that the day will come when all tears will be wiped from their eyes and that, in the meantime everything that has any positive value in the order of being is already being stored up in an eternal dwelling.

To the man of action who is perhaps concerned by the apparent pessimism of this view and the defeatism that it might engender, I would like to say, in the first place, that it is nevertheless the truth and that all truth is, per se, liberating; secondly that history shows many examples of insane cruelties committed by those in power when they believed that the gates of the perfect city were about to be opened to them as the direct result of their own work. Utopias engender tyranny and terror. And last of all, and most important, I would like to remind him that the ardor of our hope is not determined by the empirically observable results of our action but by the divine promise.

Surely the fact that torture is being used all over again—which is an undeniable fact—does not prevent us from fighting it with all the arms at our disposal? Are we not obliged to react to the circumstances with which history confronts us simply because we do live in the temporal dimension? The problems are there and we cannot ignore their pressing summons; evil and pain can no longer be endured; we must act and what action can we take except to attempt to introduce something of the absolute values of justice, peace, brotherhood and love, into the city of man?

It is not easy to be a man. It is relatively easy to glimpse the value we are aiming for, on the far horizon of a vista stretching out to infinity. It is far more difficult to come close to it and to infuse all our actions with it. If it were only a question of struggling against the weight of inertia of the human condition and of combating our own infidelity, mediocrity and sin . . . But the complexity of the reality against which we must react is such that it is not easy—in fact it is not normally possible—to estimate the exact impact of a decision, a gesture or an undertaking. Even if it were not for the inevitable blindness caused by our passions, the limited information available to us and our own lack of skills give a particular orientation to our actions and, thereby, radically relativize our quest for the absolute.

Following St. Augustin we have already emphasized the unrelenting ferocity of quarrels between men of good will over concrete problems. They all defend the very real values which they believe are being compromised and are indifferent to those they cannot see or understand. It is particularly distressing when these struggles take place amongst the faithful of the same Church united in the same faith but enclosed, each within his own limitations, and who cannot agree on the practical conclusions that should be drawn. One cannot help but feel a good deal of impatience when one sees this or has to suffer from it. Hence the quarrels and struggles which have never ceased to divide Christians ever since the first centuries and which have been a continual scandal to the pagans.

But one must recognize that these divisions necessarily flow from man's present condition: whatever may be our teaching of inchoative eschatology we can be sure that we are not yet risen, the day has not yet come when we shall know as we are known. For the time being our dwelling is still imperfect (1 Co 13:12). There is no practical political theory that can be drawn direct from Holy Scripture, no social program that can be deduced analytically from the teachings of theology: that would be far too easy.

At this point we would do well to meditate in far greater depth on the close relation between the mystery of history and the mystery of our own freedom: the Creator has chosen to endow man with this essential attribute which constitutes his honor and nobility. Faith cannot ease us of the sometimes fearful burden of free will. Revelation and the Church's teaching simply state the final end

toward which all our actions, the whole of our life, must be ordered
and lays down some very general principles which are not normally
sufficient to prescribe our practical behavior. Once our conscience is
informed it is up to us to use our own free will to decide and to act.
Our options take place in an atmosphere of tragedy as though in a
dark night illumined only from time to time by pinpoints of light
from different directions. At grips with the concrete conditions of an
extremely complex reality, man is torn between contradictory summons which seem to reach him with equal force. In order to make
his choice he has to muster all his resources of reason and culture
and exploit all the potentialities of his own human nature to their
utmost limits. But the Christian also knows that he is never left entirely to his own devices: he is able to count on the help of grace
and the gift of Council from the Spirit.

However hard we try and whatever gifts of grace and nature we
have received we must know that the final results of our action will
necessarily show a certain percentage of failure, whether on the level
of our own, personal action or, on the collective level, on the scale
of the whole of civilization. Our action always slides away from the
curve with which we had hoped to make it conform. This failure,
as failure, will always be a painful experience and all the more
deeply felt by someone who looks at the supernatural dimension of
reality for it adds to the debt that must be redeemed. But no failure
we meet with in our temporal adventure, however great, can lead
us to despair as a pagan who sees all his resources exhausted can be
led to despair. Our hope looks farther. Our institutions will always
be ambiguous and imperfect, our civilizations abortive and condemned to die. But God never promised that we would complete
the ordering of the secular city (it is significant in this respect, that
orthodox Christian teaching finally rejected the millenarist hope—
the reign of the just, with Christ, in this carnal world and within
the temporal dimension—as illusory). On the contrary we would be
better advised to expect just the opposite if we are to judge by the
imagery of the Prophets who have been inspired to evoke the Last
Days. As St. Augustine warns us, "No one should promise himself

that which the Gospel itself does not promise . . . Our Holy Scriptures announce only trials, torments, unhappiness, pain and temptation in these times" (*Enarr.* in Ps 39:28).

But, in the meantime, we have learned that true history, the history which has meaning, is not accomplished in the space-time that can be empirically observed: "For there is no eternal city for us in this life but we look for one in the life to come" (He 13:14). A deeper experience of failure should make us doubly impatient with our limits. Whatever happens, as long as we avoid the pharisaic illusions that tempt us in misleading moments of prosperity, we can never feel entirely at ease in the secular city. Its failure, its radical imperfection, the illusory character of its fleeting, partial triumphs . . . all this only goes to make us feel, all the more strongly, that "for us, our (true) homeland is in heaven, and from heaven comes the Savior we are waiting for, the Lord Jesus Christ, and he will transfigure these wretched bodies of ours into copies of his glorious body. He will do this by that same power with which he can subdue the whole universe" (Ph 3:20). Faithful to the tradition of the first generations of Christians, St. Augustine encourages us to "love and wait for the return of the Savior" (Ep. 199, 1[1], 5[14]). And so the theology of history opens onto a spirituality of the *Marana tha*: "Amen; come, Lord Jesus. May the grace of the Lord Jesus be with you all." (Rv 22:20b–21). Holy Scripture concludes with these two verses.